Y0-DBL-764

Studies in International Relations

Edited by
Charles MacDonald
Florida International University

A Routledge Series

STUDIES IN INTERNATIONAL RELATIONS

CHARLES MACDONALD, *General Editor*

PROMOTING WOMEN'S RIGHTS
The Politics of Gender in the European Union
Chrystalla A. Ellina

TURKISH FOREIGN POLICY AND TURKISH IDENTITY
A Constructivist Approach
Yücel Bozdaglioglu

ORGANIZING THE WORLD
The United States and Regional Cooperation in Asia and Europe
Galia Press-Barnathan

HUMAN RIGHTS IN CUBA, EL SALVADOR AND NICARAGUA
A Sociological Perspective on Human Rights Abuse
Mayra Gómez

NEGOTIATING THE ARCTIC
The Construction of an International Region
E.C.H. Keskitalo

THE COMMON FISHERIES POLICY IN THE EUROPEAN UNION
A Study in Integrative and Distributive Bargaining
Eugénia da Conceição-Heldt

MALAYSIA AND THE DEVELOPMENT PROCESS
Globalization Knowledge Transfers and Postcolonial Dilemmas
Vanessa C. M. Chio

INTERNATIONAL ENVIRONMENTAL TREATIES AND STATE BEHAVIOR
Factors Influencing Cooperation

Denise K. DeGarmo

Routledge
New York & London

Published in 2005 by
Routledge
270 Madison Avenue
New York, NY 10016
www.routledge-ny.com

Published in Great Britain by
Routledge
2 Park Square
Milton Park, Abingdon
Oxon OX14 4RN
www.routledge.co.uk

10 9 8 7 6 5 4 3 2

Library of Congress Cataloging-in-Publication Data

DeGarmo, Denise K., 1956-
  International environmental treaties and state behavior : factors influencing cooperation / Denise K. DeGarmo.
     p. cm. -- (Studies in international relations)
  Includes bibliographical references and index.
  ISBN 0-415-97181-0 (hardback : alk. paper)
  1. Environmental policy--International cooperation. I. Title. II. Studies in international relations (Routledge (Firm))

GE170.D445 2004
363.7'0526--dc22   2004018123

In loving memory of
Harold K. Jacobson

Industrialism is the systematic exploitation of wasting assets. In all too many cases, the thing we call progress is merely an acceleration in the rate of that exploitation. Such prosperity as we have known up to the present is the consequence of rapidly spending the planet's irreplaceable capital.

Sooner or later mankind will be forced by the pressure of circumstances to take concerted action against its own destructive and suicidal tendencies. The longer such action is postponed, the worse it will be for all concerned . . . Overpopulation and erosion constitute a Martian invasion of the planet . . . Treat Nature aggressively, with greed and violence and incomprehension: wounded Nature will turn and destroy you . . . if presumptuously imagining that we can "conquer" Nature, we continue to live on our planet like a swarm of destructive parasites—we condemn ourselves and our children to misery and deepening squalor and the despair that finds expression in the frenzies of collective violence.

—Aldous Huxley (1948) *'Managing' The Double Crises*

Contents

List of Tables

List of Appendices

Acknowledgments

I would like to dedicate this work to the memory of Professor Harold K. Jacobson. Professor Jacobson's dedication to graduate and undergraduate education inspired me to become the scholar I am today. His intellectual support allowed me to explore the depths of my intellectual curiosity while his emotional support helped me to develop confidence in my scholarship. Without his guidance, I could not have successfully completed this project. His final insights into this project were sorely missed. I also wish to thank Professor Paul Huth for his patience, encouragement, and willingness to challenge me intellectually. I would like to thank Professor Douglas Lemke for jumping in at the last minute to ensure this project would be completed on time and Professor Steven Brechin for his willingness to take on this project. A special thank you is extended to Professor Richard L. Hall for his wisdom, emotional support and valued friendship. On a more personal level, I wish to thank Jose Raul Perales-Hernandez for his friendship, willingness to engage in countless hours of conversation, and for reminding me there was a light at the end of the tunnel. I would also like to thank Lili Kivisto and Rene Lewis for their encouragement and prayers. My deepest gratitude, however, goes out to my sons who have sacrificed so much in order for me to pursue my educational dreams. Their unconditional love and support has inspired me in ways that words cannot describe.

Chapter One
International Environmental Problems and International Environmental Politics: An Overview

> In the dust where we have buried the silent races and their abominations, we have buried so much of the delicate magic of life.
>
> —D.H. Lawrence (at Taos)

The purpose of this chapter is to provide the reader with an introduction to international environmental problems and politics. The chapter is divided into four sections. The first section is devoted to a discussion of international environmental problems and their influence on state behavior in the international system. The second section examines international environmental cooperation, while the third section looks at international environmental politics. Finally, section four provides an overview of the organization of this book.

INTERNATIONAL EVIRONMENTAL PROBLEMS

Environmental Interdependence

While environmental issues have always been an important part of international relations, not until the *United Nations Stockholm Conference on the Human Environment* in 1972 were growing international concerns regarding the impact of environmental degradation on the human population and the international ramifications of the depletion of finite resources first voiced. As a result of the *Stockholm Conference,* not only did the international community recognize the collective responsibility of all states for the preservation of the earth and its biosphere, concerns regarding the nature and scope of international environmental problems have taken on increasing importance in the international arena.

However, it was not until June 1992, at the *United Nations Conference on Environment and Development,* that the international community officially recognized the transboundary or interdependent nature of environmental degradation and the subsequent implications for international security. Environmental decline was no longer considered a problem simply for local governments, but one of international concern. The importance of the ecosystems became apparent. The human population was changing the basic physiology of the planet. Over-exploitation of natural resources was exacting a toll on the availability of finite resources. If left unchecked, environmental damage would be irreversible.

Although the environment has been recognized as a critical component of national and international security, growing environmental interdependence has made it more difficult for states to insulate themselves from international environmental problems in the same way they have traditionally protected themselves with regard to military matters. The extent of military interdependence has historically vacillated according to variations in the structure of the international system and according to the individual interests of states within that system. Environmental interdependence, on the other hand, has been a consistent characteristic of the international system.

International environmental problems, therefore, have not only become a potential common adversary across the globe, they have become a common threat to every state. Not only are states unable to protect themselves from the effects of these problems, they are also incapable of resolving them without the involvement of the international community as a whole. Mutual responses to environmental problems develop only through extensive political processes and, in the end, can only be achieved through international cooperation. Therefore, international cooperation seems to be the only way in which international environmental problems may be solved. Although international cooperation may be an effective tool for resolving military problems, it is not the only tool available to states to resolve these types of problems. Other means of problem solving are also available to states including the actual use of military force or a move toward isolationism. International environmental problems, on the other hand, are different. They not only challenge the continuing existence of mankind, they cannot be resolved through coercive military tactics and strategies.

PHYSICAL DIMENSIONS OF ENVIRONMENTAL DEGRADATION

Environmental problems and conflicts are hardly a recent global phenomenon. The basic composition of the planet has undergone dramatic changes since ancient times when large numbers of people began living together in cities. Although earlier forms of environmental degradation tended to be localized in their effects, the globalization of environmental degradation can be traced as far back as 1492 with the reciprocal transatlantic invasion of flora and fauna that resulted from Christopher Columbus' exploration of the "New World."[1]

Over the course of time, considerable physical and chemical changes have taken place in the makeup of the earth's atmosphere and oceans. For instance, the change in the atmospheric concentrations of certain compounds has been identified as contributing to global climate change and the emergence of enormous holes in the ozone layer. Furthermore, genetic and biological diversity across the globe are in the process of being irreversibly eliminated. The majority of global environmental change can be directly contributed to the overwhelming growth of human activities, such as production, consumption, and disposal over the last century.[2] Global trends, such as these, help to explain the current decline of the earth's environmental stability.

INTERNATIONAL ENVIRONMENTAL COOPERATION

Collective political response to international environmental problems has become increasingly widespread during the past thirty years. Hurrell and Kingsbury define international environmental politics as:

> the processes by which inter-state agreements on the environment are negotiated; the rules and regimes established to facilitate environmental cooperation; the international institutions that have been, or need to be, created to implement those rules; and the conflicting political forces on whose resolution any successful regional or global environmental initiatives must depend.[3]

Therefore, one might envision international environmental politics as a combination of environmental issues and international politics. In approaching international environmental problems, the international community may employ a variety of strategies and mechanisms to deal with important global environmental problems. The most common approach appears to be that of international cooperation.

Achieving cooperation among members of the international community consists of two stages: 1) recognition among states that there is a need for cooperation; and, 2) negotiation between states to reach a cooperative solution. The first stage concentrates on how states come to recognize the need for cooperation. Cooperation is initially pursued by states already aware of a specific problem in order to promote international recognition of that problem. In order to increase international "awareness" it may be necessary for states to engage in the accumulation and sharing of scientific knowledge of the problem and its potential consequences. Efforts are then turned toward building an international consensus on the causes and possible solutions for the problem under scrutiny. Once these objectives have been realized and international action deemed necessary, cooperative efforts move into the second or negotiating stage. In determining the appropriate response to an international environmental problem, states may choose to utilize international conventions, international summits or international laws to address the environmental problem at hand.

Although states may recognize the need for cooperative undertakings to adequately address international environmental problems, it is also important to realize that international cooperation may be impeded by a variety of additional factors. For example, international cooperation may obstruct a state's economic development. It might also impinge upon a state's sovereignty over its territory, natural resources, and/or population. Therefore, even if states agree that cooperation and negotiation are necessary to address an international environmental problem, this does not necessarily mean that all states will become parties to or comply with such an agreement.

INTERNATIONAL ENVIRONMENTAL POLITICS

Over the past several decades, there has been a significant increase in environmental problems across the globe. Although these problems have historically been treated as domestic affairs by governments, the increasingly transboundary nature of environmental problems has resulted in these problems being incorporated into the international agenda. Environmental problems have moved beyond environmental dilemmas associated with shared borders and resources. They currently involve global ramifications stemming from the actions of each state in the world.

As international environmental problems have grown in magnitude, international environmental politics has also expanded to confront these problems. Unfortunately, political momentum has been outpaced by the intensification of environmental problems in recent years. Even further behind the political momentum has been the theoretical study of international environmental politics.

As a field of study, international environmental politics emerged approximately twenty-five years ago. The field of international environmental politics began as issue-specific studies that focused their attention on such subjects as the regulation of ocean resources or transboundary air pollution. With the exception of a brief surge of interest following the *United Nations*

Conference on the Human Environment in 1972, the field of international environmental politics received little attention from international relations scholars until the 1980s when full-fledged environmental regimes and institutions emerged. Although its history is relatively short, international environmental politics is an expanding area of study that appears to be in the process of asserting itself permanently among the top three fundamental areas of international relations theory.[4]

Thus far, however, the field of international environmental politics has been predominantly policy-oriented and has focused on problem-solving concerns, such as how to best achieve consensus and cooperation over specific environmental issues, or how to design norms, enforce laws, and monitor progress. Although scholars in the field of international environmental politics believe that there is an appropriate role for international relations theory in analyzing global environmental concerns,[5] the existing literature is predominantly descriptive or prescriptive rather than analytical.[6] The analytical work that has been done ". . . has been limited to the institutionalist vein, with little work presented from the neo-realist camp."[7] Little if any of the literature has attempted to bring environmental issues into the core of international relations theory. Only now are some scholars conducting empirical analyses to determine the useful of existing theoretical constructs in explaining state behavior in the international environmental realm.

Thus, in writing this book, I hope to further this endeavor by conducting an empirical analysis, using a combination of variables drawn from international relations theory, in order to determine their usefulness and accuracy in explaining state behavior in regard to international environmental treaties. Specifically, I will analyze the relationship between structural characteristics, economic considerations, environmental treaty types, governmental types and the probability states will become parties to international environmental treaties with time. The importance of exploring this question lies in the fact that as international environmental treaties have become the main tool through which states in the international system address environmental concerns,[8] identification of those factors that enhance the likelihood of states becoming a party to international environmental treaties will allow their inclusion in future negotiations and thus ensure a better record of state participation international environmental treaties in the future.

ORGANIZATION OF THE BOOK

This book consists of seven chapters. Chapter One introduces the reader to international environmental problems and international environmental politics. In Chapter Two, I review existing theoretical approaches to international relations and the ability of such approaches to explain state behavior in the realm of international environmental politics. Chapter Three explores the historical and analytical context of international behavior in the environmental realm. Using the partial explanations provided by an intensive review of existing international relations theory and historical experiences of states in the international environmental realm, Chapter Four not only provides a justification for this study, it discusses the data-making procedures and methodology employed in this study. Chapter Five is devoted to an analysis of my findings, while Chapter Six tests the findings of this study using a case study approach. Finally Chapter Seven provides a summary of my findings and discusses how this analysis has improved on existing studies of international environmental politics and international relations theory.

Chapter Two

International Relations Theory and International Environmental Politics: Epistemological Issues and Existing Approaches

> We are all prisoners of a rigid conception of what is important and what is not. We anxiously follow what we suppose to be important, while what we suppose to be unimportant wages guerrilla warfare behind our backs, transforming the world without our knowledge and eventually mounting a surprise attack on us.
>
> —Milan Kundera, *The Book of Laughter and Forgetting*

In this chapter, I review existing theoretical approaches to international relations and the ability of such approaches to explain state behavior in the realm of international environmental politics. This chapter is divided into two main sections. The first section examines epistemological issues of social inquiry and how they relate to international relations theory and international environmental politics. The second section is a literature review on international relations theory and international environmental politics. The conclusion acknowledges that while the literature on international relations theory and international environmental politics is plentiful and diverse, it has yet to provide a comprehensive approach to the study of both fields as one.

EPISTEMOLOGICAL ISSUES OF POLITICAL SCIENCE INQUIRY

In political science, inquiries into political phenomena require researchers to collect facts relevant to the phenomenon under examination, present this information in an analytical manner using a particular theoretical approach as a guide, and organize a set of conclusions. However, if the investigation of particular political phenomena does not fit neatly into this pattern of inquiry, it is often beneficial to examine the epistemological foundations of these approaches to see how such approaches go about procuring knowledge. The examination of international activity in regard to environmental issues is one such example of a political phenomenon not fitting neatly into existing patterns of social inquiry. Therefore, I have had to reexamine a number of epistemological issues in my study of state behavior and international environmental treaties. I begin with an evaluation of literature on international environmental politics and work backward to the foundations of international relations theory.

Attempts to utilize international relations theory as a framework for studying issues of the global environment, and more specifically, state behavior in the international environmental realm, have only recently emerged in the field of international relations, and therefore, are underdeveloped.[1] Although, scholars in the field believe that there is an appropriate role for international relations theory in analyzing international environmental politics, the existing literature is predominantly descriptive or prescriptive rather than analytical.[2] As the University of California at Los Angeles *Conference on the Social Sciences and Environment* (1992) discovered,[3] the work to date is characterized by "limited research in the institutionalist vein with little from the neorealist camp."[4] The predominant approach to international environmental problems, then, has been regime theory, which aims at resolving problems of international cooperation in the environmental realm rather than the feasibility of the political arrangements that allowed cooperation to occur in the first place. Based on this assessment, a better understanding of international environmental relations will require a more thorough examination of existing theoretical constructs to evaluate their ability to explain state behavior in this sphere. Thus, before examining the literature relevant to my subject matter, I will explore some of the epistemological issues of international relations theory in general.

In order to contribute to the existing knowledge of any field in the social sciences, researchers must first decide what question or questions they want to examine. Then, they must decide on what theoretical approach to utilize in the study of the phenomenon of interest. While these decisions may appear straightforward on the surface, one must remember that the epistemological characteristics of social science are quite complex in many respects. First, the units of analyses in the social sciences do not exhibit a predetermined response to comparable social conditions. In other words, each unit of analysis has distinctive characteristics that influence their response to external stimuli. Therefore, no two units are exactly the same and cannot be expected to respond to similar social conditions in a like manner. Additionally, experiments in the social sciences cannot be as precisely constructed or controlled as experiments in the natural sciences—experiments in the social sciences cannot be conducted in the sterile atmosphere of a laboratory. Finally, it has been argued that the social sciences can not achieve the same level of objectivity as the natural sciences because the biases and particular interests of the researcher tend to influence not only his/her research agenda, but are reflected in the accumulation of "knowledge" itself. Given the complexity of social science inquiry, then, the prediction of events with 100% confidence or the ability to fully explain or understand phenomenon is limited no matter how well constructed the epistemological foundations or methodology are.

International Relations Theory and International Environmental Politics: Irreconcilable Differences?

The field of International Relations is currently undergoing a transformation as major changes in the international arena have challenged the traditional approaches to inquiry and explanation.[5] Although the field was never completely unified in its approach, the rate of changes across the international landscape has resulted in an even more diverse field of study. Explanations of international relations range from the deterministic laws of neorealism to the rebellious voices of postmodernism.

Among the more traditional theoretical approaches in the field of International Relations, neorealism and neoliberalism vie for primacy. Neorealism,[6] on the one hand, says little about environmental issues and provides a rather discouraging view regarding the prospects for cooperation between states. Neoliberalism, on the other hand, addresses international environmental problems and presents an optimistic view regarding the prospects for cooperation between states.

Neither of these views of international relations, though, is entirely new. The foundations of neoliberalism, and more specifically regime theory, can be traced to works that emerged in the 1970s on the subject of economic interdependence between states—most notably Robert Keohane and Joseph Nye's book entitled *Power and Interdependence* (1977).[7] International relations scholars, however, did not create the concept of ecological interdependence. Rather, it spread from the scientific and environmental fields into the literature on international relations. With the increased importance given to environmental issues in the international arena and the proliferation of new institutions and treaties to address them, scholars in the field of international relations began publishing an impressive number of articles and books on the subject.

Initially, the literature dealt with subjects such as the role of institutions and regimes in achieving cooperation between states and how more effective cooperation could be achieved in order to resolve international environmental problems.[8] To the extent these works incorporated fragments of international relations theory, they did so using a regime theoretical or the closely related approach of "liberal institutionalism."

Regime theory literature has provided important insights into state behavior in the international environmental realm by: 1) specifying the context within which actors make choices; 2) identifying strategies and mechanisms by which states could achieve cooperative behavior in the international arena; and, 3) enabling descriptions of patterns of cooperation. Despite the importance of this knowledge, critics of regime theory argue that this perspective fails to adequately address: 1) the structural constraints that prevent regimes from having significant influence on state action, global peace and security; 2) the influence of power configurations on regime formation, agenda setting, and policy formulation; 3) cooperation that occurs outside the boundaries of regimes; 4) influences that motivate states to become parties to international environmental treaties; and, 5) differences in state behavior despite the presence of regimes. Hence, critics argue that regime theory's "policy orientation" limits its attention to questions of epistemology or methodology, let alone the development of a full-fledged theory of international relations.[9] While regime theory has, for the most part, remained a distinct sub-area of international relations theory, the broader collection of literature encompassed under the rubric of neoliberalism has addressed most areas of international relations.

Meanwhile, the literature on international environmental politics tends to be apolitical. As J. Samuel Barkin and George Shambaugh point out, "theorizing about international environmental politics began with the assumption of the 'common enemy' of environmental threat or the tragedy of the commons situation that hindered international action to meet that threat."[10] The study of international environmental politics, then, became a process of finding appropriate cooperative or institutional mechanisms to overcome international environmental problems rather than addressing "the viability of the political settlement underlying the mechanisms."[11] Barkin and Shambaugh conclude that this approach is highly unrealistic because international environmental issues are as politicized as most other kinds of international issues. Ignoring this fact will make dealing with international environmental problems more difficult.

Whether based on regime theory or not, the literature on international environmental politics remains disconnected from the realist and neorealist approaches to international relations. The different approaches to international environmental problems—theories of international relations and policy prescriptions of international environmental politics—has led some scholars to conclude that the two fields of study are incompatible. So long as international environmental politics and international relations theory remain distinct fields, International Relations theorists will continue to overlook an important component of international relations. Experts in international environmental politics, on the other hand, will continue to treat their subject in isolation from major aspects of relations between states (i.e., power politics).

Therefore, I will argue that in order to gain a better understanding of state behavior in the international environmental realm, international environmental politics must be incorporated into the heart of international relations theory in order to create a comprehensive framework for inquiry and explanation. In order to accomplish this, I will draw on explanatory variables from various strands of international relations theory and evaluate their usefulness in explaining state behavior in the sphere of international environmental conventions through empirical testing.

International Relations Theory: Traditional and Supplementary Approaches

Neoliberalism and neorealism are distinct theoretical explanations in the study of international relations. However, they do share a common characteristic: they are both structural approaches. In other words, they do not attempt to look inside states for explanations for state behavior. Rather, they examine external influences to states such as geopolitical power structures and institutional structures, to explain state behavior. Classical realism, on the other hand, focuses to a greater extent on the state as the primary actor in international relations.

Even though neorealism and classical realism identify different influences as the source of state behavior, they are often placed in the same category when it comes to the issue of cooperation. In both of these approaches, the prospects for cooperation between states are negative. Neoliberalism is placed into another category in which the prospects for cooperation are positive. The one characteristic that all three theoretical approaches share is the primacy of the state as the unit of analysis. This characteristic differentiates these approaches from the others that will be presented here. One final note, only one of these three approaches gives attention to environmental issues—neoliberalism.

International Relations Theory, Non-State Actors, and Internal Attributes

Other approaches to the fields of international relations and international environmental politics focus on domestic level or internal characteristics of states as the source of state behavior in the international arena. While incorporating non-state actors[12] into any explanation of state behavior in the international arena challenges the parsimony of state-centric approaches; actors at the domestic level have been an important source of influence in international environmental policymaking.[13]

The literature on non-state actors examines their contributions in assisting states with: 1) agenda setting; 2) establishing consensus; 3) devising monitoring schemes; and, 4) achieving cooperation in the international setting. Non-state actors, operating in this capacity, can be seen as working within the state system and therefore can be incorporated into the study of international relations.

While many non-state actors pursue environmental protection as their primary goal, there are also numerous groups (i.e., interest groups, organizations and businesses) whose purpose is to impede the development of new environmental constraints on their activities. Literature discussing the role of groups such as these is virtually non-existent in the field of international relations.

In addition to non-state actors, the influences of internal attributes of states often enter into discussions of international relations. As illustrated in the literature on "Democratic Peace,"[14] internal attributes (in this approach the internal attribute is the type of political system) can provide an explanation of state behavior in the international arena.

While all of these factors may be important to any discussion of international relations, it is also important to mention that non-state actors and internal attributes cannot create international law or policy by themselves. It is ultimately up to the state to chart its own course of action. As Karen Liftin observes:

> ... only states have the human and financial resources to mount large-scale scientific and technical projects for detecting, monitoring, and preserving the global environment. Only the state, at the intersection of domestic international politics, has sufficient authority, political legitimacy, and territorial control to influence the causal agents of deterioration. [15]

The primary focus of the literature review that follows will be on the mainstream theoretical approaches to international relations and international environmental politics. It will also briefly look at some of the more peripheral approaches to international relations (i.e., epistemic communities, security issues of the environment, and social constructivism).

LITERATURE REVIEW

Classical Realism and Its Variations

There are three main approaches to the study of international relations and international environmental politics. The state-centric approach is one such method whereby the primary unit of analysis is the state. This approach does not look at other units or levels of analysis for the purpose of explanation. Classical realism is a prime example of this approach.[16]

The underlying assumptions of classical realism are: 1) states are the principle actors in international relations; 2) the state is a unitary actor; 3) the state is a rational actor; and, 4) state behavior in the international arena is determined by national security issues which revolve around issues of power. Furthermore, according to classical realism, the international system is characterized as anarchic. Given these assumptions, then, the state seeks to maximize its power position in the international system, which results in conflictive rather than cooperative behavior between states.

Even though some realists were willing to consider the environment as an international security concern after the *United Nations Conference on the Human Environment (UNCHE)* in 1972, the prevailing belief among realists is the environment is distinct from security concerns and of far less importance to the state. As Lynton Caldwell notes: "Perceived national interest rather than the Stockholm Declaration of Principles or the interventions of UNEP has been the prime mover of international environmental cooperation."[17]

In addition to the assumptions provided by classical realism, states are unlikely to cooperate in the international arena due to relative gains concerns associated with the structural constraints of an anarchic international system.[18] According to this view, survival is the driving force of state behavior and survival in the international system is dependent upon the relative capabilities of states. Since states are positional, they are concerned with cheating and the gain partners make in cooperative efforts because those gains may be ultimately used against them in future encounters. In order to maintain their position in the international system, then, states may seek to prevent gains in other states' relative capabilities. As Rodney White notes, states are unwilling to make any concessions that they fear will disadvantage them in the world system.[19] With a focus on relative gains, states perceive their interactions with other states as zero-sum interactions. So, even though the international environmental movement gained strength and momentum in the 1970s and beyond, many scholars of the classical realist tradition maintained that in an anarchic system, the sovereign state is the most serious roadblock to achieving the cooperation necessary to address international environmental concerns.

As the environment takes on increasing importance in the international system, a growing body of literature has emerged within the realist approach that incorporates the environment into security concerns. This allows the main assumptions of classical realism to stay intact and the increasing importance of environmental issues is not ignored.

The work of Thomas Homer-Dixon has been paramount in identifying the correlation between resource scarcity and conflict.[20] According to Homer-Dixon, the depletion of natural resources decreases the economic resources available for local and national governmental use. The inability of the state to produce adequate revenues weakens the overall administrative capacity and authority of the government, leading to an increase in the demands placed upon the state. The resulting economic and political stresses associated with the depletion of natural resources may greatly weaken the state and create opportunities for violent challenges to the state by political and military opponents.[21] Therefore, as environmental problems become more severe, they may precipitate civil and international strife.

The work of the *World Commission on Environment and Development (WCED)* supported Homer-Dixon's conclusions. The Commission found that states often fight each other to assert and resist control over raw materials, energy supplies, land, river basins, and sea passages. As environmental stress increases as a result of resource depletion, conflict increases. Therefore, environmental stress causes and effects political tension and military conflict.[22]

The link between environmental degradation, resource depletion, and conflict also found support in the work of Arthur Westing. Although they are only a small fraction of the overall number of international militarized disputes, Westing was able to identify eight international conflicts that involved a natural resource component: 1) World War I (1914–1918); 2) the Chaco War (1932–1935); 3) World War II (1939–1945); 4) the Third Arab-Israeli War (1967); 5) the El-Salvador-Honduras War (1969); 6) the Anglo-Icelandic Clash (1972–1973); 7) the Parcel Island Clash (1974); and, 8) the Falkland-Malvinas Conflict (1982).[23]

Homer-Dixon also identified another important consequence of environmental scarcity—the shift in the international balance of power. As environmental scarcity worsens, the gap between rich and poor countries increases. This leads to a confrontation between rich and poor countries over the more equitable distribution of wealth. While this shift could take place regionally or globally, the final results would still be the same—increased international instability.[24]

On the one hand, environmental issues appear conformant to security issues. On the other hand, critics argue that some theorists are using the security issue as a means to preserve their theories. Therefore, not all theorists believe that the environment and security should be linked together as one issue. Hugh Dyer is one such theorist who argues against the incorporation of the environment into traditional security issues. According to Dyer, the international environment should not be subjugated to the traditional political-military security agenda, but rather should be valued on its own terms. Incorporation disregards the importance of environmental issues in other respects, such as the implications of environmental degradation on future generations.[25]

Another way in which realists have addressed the environment without compromising their theoretical framework has been by treating the environment as an economic good. According to this view, states will "generally allocate rights to extract or protect resources in ways that benefit the state itself."[26] Therefore, despite the willingness of states to recognize international environmental problems, any collective action on the global environment "will have to be achieved with little or no net loss in a participating nation's economic competitiveness."[27] If the environment is valued as an economic good, then, states may engage in cooperative behavior.

In order to change state behavior toward the environment, scholars argue that market-based incentives should be applied to environmental goods.[28] Environmental externalities,[29] whether in terms of costs (i.e., pollution) or benefits (i.e. creation of new habitats), are by-products of all economic activities. Since environmental externalities are not factored into market costs or prices, there is little incentive for environmentally sound economic activities. If this trend were reversed, and the value of environmental externalities were incorporated into actual market costs and prices, scholars argue that the economic system would correct itself by providing the necessary incentives for activities that are environmentally beneficial. Environmental activities that are costly would be avoided.

While there is increased recognition among the international community that environmental goods do have an economic value,[30] these goods continue to be undervalued by the failure of traditional economic measurement techniques to incorporate them into overall economic performance.[31] This trend may be reversing. As of 1993, the United Nations' system of national accounts began to include a greater number of environmental factors: 1) natural resource wealth; 2) renewable resource depletion; and, 3) wealth of mineral stocks.

Scholars also point out that if an environmental externality is easily identifiable, states are more likely to make the appropriate adjustments in their economic activities. If states can agree on the value of the externality, then the value can be offset through the transfer of economic or technological resources. The transfer of economic and/or technology occurs for the purpose of: 1) compensating the recipient state for the provision of an international environmental good or service; and, 2) to help mitigate the unequal relative costs of environmental protection from one country to another. While this approach provides useful insight into state behavior in the international environmental realm, for the most part this work is rooted in policy proposals rather than empirical facts.[32]

While many scholars dismiss classical realism as an appropriate theoretical approach through which to examine international environmental relations,[33] little if any evidence beyond mere assertion is presented to support this claim. Furthermore, many of those same scholars recognize that sovereignty and the pursuit of national interests create barriers to cooperation, which is necessary for effective international agreements. Eric Eckholm notes that when states' "immediate economic and political interests are affected, national governments have proved unwilling to grant significant powers to international authority."[34] Immanuel Wallerstein further argues that sovereign states are the defining feature of the modern world system. Therefore, according to Wallerstein, regimes are unable to deal effectively with emerging international crises because they consist of sovereign states, are designed to serve state interests, and reflect the existing power distribution of the international system.[35]

While classical realism, in its original incarnation, failed to discuss the behavior of states in the international environmental realm, it is reasonable to assume that realism and its modified versions may provide useful insights regarding structural characteristics and their influence on state behavior in the international environmental realm. Within this theoretical framework, states would be expected to become parties to international environmental agreements when it is in their national interest to do so—when an international environmental agreement furthers or does not compromise the national security or power of a given state in the international system. Realism would also suggest states would become parties to an international environmental agreement when the environment is valued as an economic good.

Neorealism and Neoliberalism

Although neoliberalism and neorealism focus on the structural characteristics of the international system as the basis of state behavior, they are distinctive theoretical approaches in the study of international relations. Neorealism proposes that anarchy creates an international system characterized by self-help and the security dilemma. As the primary goal of states, survival limits cooperation because states fear exploitation. Therefore, competition rather than cooperation is the norm of behavior in relationships between states.

Neoliberalism, while supporting the notion that anarchy does influence state behavior in the international system, proposes that increasing interdependence provides an alternative structural context in which states define their interests and coordinate their conflicting policies through international institutions and regimes.

In addition to a discussion of neorealism and neoliberalism, this section will examine the literature that promotes the replacement of the anarchical international system with a more hierarchical one through the negotiation of international law and the establishment of a supra-national authority.

Neorealism

Neorealism analyzes how the structure of the international system conditions the behavior of states. According to this approach, the state resides in an international community based on anarchy or the absence of authority above the state. Since there is no supra-national authority above the state to ensure its security, each state must rely upon its own capabilities to guarantee its security and survival. Therefore, the international system is a self-help system. Anarchy and self-help create a condition known as the security dilemma, or the inability of states to be confident that gains in relative capabilities (be it weapons, power, or the such) will not be used against them in future encounters. Since survival in the system is dependent upon a state's relative capabilities or power, states will pursue their national interests in ways that not only maintain their power position but also prevent gains in other state's relative capabilities. Therefore, behavior in the international system is more likely to be competitive or conflictual rather than cooperative.

The underlying assumptions of neorealism are: 1) the state is the most important organization in international relations; 2) states are self interested; 3) states are rational, unitary actors seeking to survive in an international system characterized by anarchy; 4) states pursue goals based on their national interest irrespective of their form of government and economic organization; and, 5) the accumulation of power ensures state survival in the international system.

While these assumptions may appear similar to those of classical realism, neorealists argue that classical realism relies on reductionist explanations of state behavior by focusing on the foreign policies and external behaviors of states rather than examining the influence of structural or systemic characteristics. Classical realism, then, cannot account for consistency in state behavior despite variation in internal attributes and in the types of interactions. The anarchical structure of the international system and the distribution of relative capabilities across states,[36] according to neorealists, account for this apparent uniformity in state behavior. Neorealism also differs from classical realism in that it makes no assumption regarding state behavior other than the state seeks survival in the international system.

While neorealists admit that the prospects for cooperation in an international system characterized by anarchy are grim, they do not deny that it does occur. When cooperation does occur, neorealists view it as a short-lived strategic maneuver[37] that will give way to competitive or conflictual strategies once systemic or structural disparities emerge in the international system. As a result of these structural changes, traditional security issues will return to the forefront of international policy agendas, while international issues requiring cooperative solutions, such as international environmental problems, will be placed on the "back burner."

As is the case with realism, neo-realism does not specifically mention the effects of structural characteristics on state behavior in the international environmental sphere. Despite this shortcoming, it seems reasonable to assume that within this theoretical framework state behavior in regard to the international environment would be dictated by the desire of states to maintain their power position in the international system in order to survive within that system. Therefore, states are likely to become parties to international environmental treaties when impending environmental degradation threatens the survival of the state or such a treaty does not alter the state's relative power position in the international system.

Neoliberalism

Neoliberalism recognizes that in addition to an anarchical international system, growing interdependence[38] between states limits the prospects for cooperation. According to Hempel, growing interdependence between states is the result of: 1) advances in information technology and global communication; 2) rapid growth in population and migration; 3) heightened risks of terrorism and nuclear proliferation; and, 4) accelerating rates of transboundary pollution and nonrenewable resource consumption.[39] Hempel also suggests that as a result of increased interdependence, the asymmetrical properties of the relationships between states are growing stronger in some areas (i.e., increased gap between rich and poor countries). Hempel concludes that asymmetries not only account for "inequities in the allocation rules that govern international trade, development and use of global commons; they may also inhibit cooperation needed for coordinated responses to global environmental change."[40]

Hence, in response to the bleak assessment of cooperation presented in the neorealist and interdependence literature, neoliberalists argue that even under these conditions, cooperation between states can be achieved through international institutions and regimes. Neoliberalism, then, examines the role of international institutions, organizations, and regimes in structuring the interactions between states within the international system. This approach is the one traditional theory of international relations that addresses international environmental issues.

The underlying assumptions of neoliberalism are: 1) states are atomistic actors; 2) the driving force of state behavior in the international system is the maximization of individual absolute gains or achieving the greatest gains regardless of gains made by others; 3) cheating is the greatest barrier to international cooperation; and, 4) international institutions and regimes provide strategies and mechanisms through which states can reduce the probability of cheating and increase the probability of cooperation.

Studies of international organizations have traditionally focused on cooperative behavior among states. While organizational theorists characterize states as rational and unitary actors, they do not insist that the state is necessarily the most important actor in the international system. Rather, international organizations are the central arenas in which international politics occur and are studied. With the increasing importance attached to environmental issues by the international community and the necessity of international cooperation to solve these problems, the study of international institutions has been reinvigorated.

Oran Young's "institutional bargaining" approach, one such example of this line of inquiry, explores state behavior within multilateral organizations.[41] According to Young, institutional bargaining is a process whereby states interact to produce an agreement that governs their behavior in a specific issue area. Unlike ordinary provisions of international governance, institutional bargaining uses consensus to provide states with an incentive to create rules and norms of behavior that are attractive to as many interests as possible.[42] In this way, meaningful agreements can be reached that appear equitable to all parties.

Closely associated with the study of international institutions, regime theory focuses on the role of regimes in managing interstate conflict and solving collective action problems. A regime is defined as "explicit principles, norms, rules and decision making procedures around which actor's expectations converge in a given issue area."[43] According to this theoretical approach, regimes facilitate international cooperation under anarchy by: 1) increasing communication between states; 2) increasing the shadow of the future; 3) increasing iteration through the decomposition of moves; 4) monitoring state behavior; 5) issue linkage; 6) increasing information which decreases uncertainty and asymmetry (or a states ability to manipulate others because it has more information; 7) creating norms and rules for behavior; and, 8) encouraging reciprocity.[44]

The popularity of regime theory in the study of international relations lies in its ability to explain "cooperation under anarchy," while at the same time illustrating how regimes serve as "facilitators" of international cooperation. Additionally, regime theory has broad applicability to numerous issue areas within the field of international relations.

The need for cooperative strategies and solutions to international environmental problems made regime theory a popular approach to the study of international environmental politics. A plethora of regimes have emerged to address a variety of international environmental problems, including global warming, biodiversity, the oceans, and ozone depletion. The regime approach not only enables the researcher to focus his/her attention on one issue at a time, thus enhancing one's understanding of the issue, it provides an opportunity to compare and contrast regime formation across time and issue areas. Thus, a better understanding of the role of regimes in the international environment could provide valuable insights in addressing these problems in the future.

In sum, neoliberalism proposes that increased international environmental concerns are generating new forms of political activity beyond the state. In other words, states cooperate to cope with international environmental problems by creating international regimes and organizations. By lowering transaction costs and providing monitoring mechanisms, states are more likely to participate in international environmental agreements that come under the supervision of such an organization. But as Karen Liftin notes, while international environmental concerns may indeed be creating new forms of political activity beyond the state, "states remain the key players within new international institutions."[45] Therefore,

> International organizations and regimes are only as important as their most powerful members wish them to be. They are institutions created by states to further their interests and are bound by the prevailing distribution of state power. Structural constraints prevent them from having significant influence on state action and on global peace and security.[46]

International Law and Supranational Authority

Despite instances of cooperation among states and the presence of international organizations and regimes, some scholars continue to argue that in an anarchical international system, sovereign states cannot produce the levels of cooperation necessary to protect the environment from impending crises. In this way, these scholars share the belief of more traditional realists that international environmental problems are incompatible with the state system. In contrast to realism, though, these scholars propose the replacement of the anarchical international system with a more hierarchical one through the creation of international law and supra-national authority.[47] Without some higher authority to oversee the activities of states, the "tragedy of the commons" is unavoidable.

The *Declaration of the Hague* (1989) was one such attempt to create a supra-national authority to deal with environmental problems of international concern. The purpose of the declaration was to create "a new, or newly strengthened, body within the United Nations that would make decisions concerning environmental issues even in the absence of unanimous agreement."[48] Signatories of the declaration saw unanimity as a major impediment for creating and implementing international agreements to protect the international environment. The declaration would force states to be bound to international agreements in the absence of unanimity. The proposed United Nations body would be able to penalize violations of existing agreements and mandate disputes to the World Court for settlement. While the declaration proposed the elimination of sovereign jurisdiction over environmental issues, it did not propose the complete elimination of state sovereignty. Hence, a hierarchical form of governance would only be established in the international environmental realm, anarchy would survive in all other areas of the international system. Unfortunately, this document is "almost universally ignored."[49]

While the creation of a supra-national entity to oversee the activities of the state, at least in the realm of the environment, might appear to be an effective way to deal with international environmental problems, it is unlikely that such an entity will gain international support any time soon.[50] First, there is no available evidence to support the claim that a supranational organization could deal more effectively and efficiently with international environmental problems. Second, the state "remains extremely resilient as a focus for human loyalties and as a structure for the exercise of political power."[51] In other words, there appears to be little support for a move toward supra-nationalism among leaders and populations of the world's states. Third, "claims about the need to abolish or limit sovereignty have to be thought through in the context of all other issues of international life."[52] Once sovereignty is relinquished in one area, it is more likely to be relinquished in others whether an appropriate response or not. Therefore, the environment should not be viewed in isolation from other international issues. Fourth, so long as material wealth and power remain key objectives of states, it is unlikely they would cede power over domestic and international decision-making to an overarching authority. As Hurrell and Kingsbury note:

> The capacity to determine the international agenda has rightly been identified as a particularly effective form of power. The industrialized countries have successfully focused international attention on those issues that affect them the most directly: marine pollution, ozone depletion, global climate change, biodiversity, and deforestation. By contrast, the states and peoples of the South have had less success in securing prominence for environmental problems closely associated with development.[53]

Finally, even if states agreed to abide by the decisions of such an entity, there is no guarantee that those decisions would be enforced.[54]

Another possible approach to international environmental cooperation by means of authoritative measures is through the creation of international environmental law. In general, international law serves several functions: 1) it is a means of communication; 2) it can clarify expectations; 3) it promotes predictability among states; 4) it can provide a framework for management and coordination; 5) it regulates conflict; 6) it can protect and enhance policy positions; and, 7) it can mobilize public support. As Jacobson and Weiss observe, international environmental law:

> has the potential to transform the ways in which humanity use the planet, the quality of lives all over the world, relations among states, the global economic system, the development paths of advanced and industrializing countries alike, and the differences between North and South.[55]

International environmental law, then, is a key mechanism by which states manage natural resources and deal with areas of common jurisdiction.

Most typically, the literature regarding international environmental law encompasses two areas: 1) a historical accounting of convention negotiation in regard to a specific issue area; and, 2) an evaluation of the two basic processes used to achieve binding solutions to international environmental problems. Here, I will provide an overview of the literature in the second area.

Scholars in both international relations and international environmental politics have begun to examine the role of international law in resolving issues of international importance. These scholars have examined the efficiency and effectiveness of processes utilized by the international community to reach binding solutions. Two approaches have been identified: 1) the one-step or comprehensive convention approach; and, 2) the two-step or framework treaty approach.

The one-step approach is characteristic of international environmental negotiations prior to the mid-1980s. States using this approach attempt to craft "all encompassing" conventions and comprehensive regimes by elucidating specific rights and responsibilities of the parties to the convention. This type of convention is often referred to as an "all-or-nothing" approach. One such an example of this approach is the *Law of the Sea.*

The second approach is known as a framework convention or two-step approach. The first step involves the establishment of general objectives, obligations and non-binding action plans of parties to the convention. The second step involves the creation of protocols that mandate specific actions to be taken by the parties to the convention. In other words, the framework convention entails a statement of agreed upon principles, the creation of mechanisms for promoting further research and data collection, and the establishment of a forum and timetable for subsequent negotiations on specific issues. The protocols emerge from the framework convention and cover in detail, specific aspects of the problem, as well as, mechanisms for regular review and revision. The conventions on climate change, ozone depletion, and biodiversity are examples of the two-step approach. According to many scholars, the framework convention is more advantageous than the one-step approach because it "makes agreement easier to obtain by bracketing off the hard decisions about precise obligations and actions."[56] In fact, the framework model has been the leading model of convention negotiation over the past ten years.

While this literature has provided a better description of the contexts in which states are more likely to cooperate, scholars admit that the negotiation of international environmental treaties is complex. First, there may be a lack of specific information necessary to formulate agreements. Second, the recommended solutions to international environmental problems may be constrained by the costs of deploying new technologies to address such problems. Third, states are concerned with equity or the fair allocation of costs associated with implementation and compliance of such treaties. Fourth, international environmental negotiations are affected by the overall climate of international relations more generally, and political rivalries more specifically.[57] Fifth, negotiations often result in an acceptance of the lowest common denominator in order to appeal to the largest number of signatory states, thus diluting the overall effect of the agreement. Sixth, there is no over-arching mechanism through which to enforce compliance with international environmental law. Seventh, negotiations focus on the allocation of losses incurred through environmental regulations not with the gains that result from wiser resource management. And, finally, states will avoid international conventions that threaten to compromise their sovereignty or hamper their national interests.[58]

In sum, the literature on international law, especially in the realm of the environment, does provide various historical accounts of convention negotiation in specific issue areas and provides an overview of the various approaches to convention construction. What is missing from this literature is a more developed discussion as to why states become parties to international environmental agreements in a more general context. This is an area in which not much is known.

Despite this apparent shortcoming in the literature, one might still infer that states are more likely to accede to: 1) framework or two-step international environmental conventions; 2) treaties negotiated on the basis of documented facts regarding the specific issue at hand; 3) treaties that provide for the fair allocation of the costs associated with implementation of the convention; and, 4) treaties that acknowledge a state's sovereign right over its resources.

Non-Governmental Actors and the Internal Attributes of States

So far in this chapter, I have reviewed the traditional approaches to international relations and international environmental politics: classical realism, neorealism, and neoliberalism. I will now review the literature that examines the influence of internal attributes and domestic actors on state behavior in realm of the international environment.

Internal Attributes of States

If realist assumptions of the state[59] are dismissed, then the exploration of a state's internal political and non-political conditions may provide valuable insights into state behavior in the international system. Explanations based on the internal attributes of the state challenge realist and neorealist conceptions. Neorealism espouses that all states are treated as like units and any internal differences should be ignored. In turn, explanations based on internal attributes argue that states will act differently under identical external conditions when internal conditions vary substantially from one state to the next. In other words, state behavior is largely determined by internal political constraints, process, and structures. Additionally, state behavior is affected by non-political characteristics such as geographic location, economic conditions, or ecological distinctiveness. While decisions of the state are still driven by national interests, national interests are expressed in terms of its internal interests according to this view.

In recent years, scholarly attention has been focused on the specific internal attribute of governmental type. Most striking is the proposed relationship between democratic governmental types and pacific behavior in the international arena.[60] If that indeed were the case, then one might infer that democratic or "more free" governmental forms might also influence state behavior in the realm of the international environment. As Gleditsch and Sverdrup assert, "[B]ecause democracies do not fight each other and usually have fairly good environmental records, then the possibilities for both peace and environmental progress are linked."[61] But as these authors also point out:

> there have been few theoretical studies and empirical investigations on the influence of the political system on environmental performance. More emphasis has been placed on the impact of the economic system, on environmental negotiations, diplomacy and formation of international regimes.[62]

Therefore, discussions involving the influence of democracy in the environmental realm are absent from literature on democracy and international relations theory, as well as international environmental politics literature.

Among attempts to explore the relationship between democracy and environment, two divergent views have emerged. The first perspective is that democracies tend to harm the environment.[63] The second viewpoint asserts that democracies perform more responsibly in the realm of the international environment because they participate more willingly in global environmental cooperation and have open markets that are a good incentive for responsible environmental policies.[64] These assertions are supported by the work of Jacobson and Weiss. They have proposed that many characteristics of democracy are conducive to a state's decision to participate in negotiations involving the international environment. These characteristics include increased transparency, importance of public opinion, and greater freedom in which non-governmental agencies can operate.[65] In addition to participation in international treaty making, these authors also found that

> because democratic societies are more likely to have powerful NGOs dedicated to environmental protection and an informed and engaged citizenry, it is not surprising that democratic countries are more likely to be in substantial compliance than those that are not democratic.[66]

Finally, in an extensive analysis of governmental performance in a diverse array of international environmental issues,[67] Gleditsch and Sverdrup found a correlation between democracy and good environmental performance except in the emission of climate gases.[68]

Despite the lack of comprehensive studies regarding governmental type and international environmental behavior, many authors cite the existence of good environmental records, the existence of a knowledgeable citizenry, and the presence of powerful NGOs as proof that democracies engage in more environmentally responsible behavior than non-democracies. Based on this assertion, then, it also seems reasonable to assume that democracies are more likely to engage in and accede to international environmental agreements than non-democracies. Additional research into the relationship between democracy and the international environment could further enhance and clarify our understanding of state behavior in the international environmental arena.

Domestic Actors

In addition to the proposed influence of internal attributes on state behavior, domestic actors are being increasingly looked upon as powerful sources of state behavior in the international realm. As Switzer notes, "NGOs play a leading role in environmental policy making in both industrialized and developing nations."[69] Specifically, I will focus my attention on the literature that examines the role of non-governmental organizations (NGOs) in the international environmental arena.

NGOs have been defined as "organizations that cut across national boundaries and are made up of individuals or national groups, not official representatives of national governments."[70] NGOs encompass such distinct groups as religious bodies, professional organizations, and, trade unions. Furthermore they may be composed of individuals or national societies that themselves are composed of individuals.[71]

Earlier work on NGOs narrowly focused on their organizational functions and influence within specific issue areas of the international system. NGOs serve several different functions. First, they can provide a means of communication and promote contact across state boundaries on issues of common interest. NGOs can often fill the vacuum left by ineffective or non-existent governmental programs or extend the reach of resource poor nations and national governments.[72] Finally, NGOs can serve as an independent voice for public participation, either in opposition to governmental programs or by placing pressures on a government to create a new program. In other words, NGOs can function as pressure groups affecting national governments or international organizations.[73] The effectiveness of NGOs, then, is in their ability to change governmental policy rather than through direct action.[74]

The incredible growth of NGOs around the world[75] and their increasing involvement in international negotiations[76] has expanded the study of NGOs to include their increasing influence in the international environmental realm. Of recent importance is the incorporation of NGOs into the study of "global governance." In this context, global governance "refers to people, political institutions, regimes, and non-governmental organizations at all levels of public and private policy making that are collectively responsible for managing world affairs."[77] As David Malin Roodman notes, NGOs are important organizing tools around which global civil society can press concerns for the international environment.[78] The scope of study on NGOs, then, has been expanded as a result of "global governance" studies to include: 1) the role of NGOs in establishing global environmental coalitions; 2) the capacity of NGOs to pressure national governments and intergovernmental institutions to initiate policy reforms; 3) the role of NGOs in providing an organizing force for constituents and communities traditionally underrepresented in the environmental decision-making process (i.e., indigenous populations); and, 4) the increasing involvement of NGOs in the process of rule-making and regime formation in the international environmental arena.[79] Based upon this literature, then, one would expect that states would be more likely to become parties to international environmental treaties when NGOs have played an active role in the negotiation of such treaties.

In addition to NGOs, there is also a growing recognition of the important role "epistemic communities" play in modifying state behavior in the international environmental realm. Epistemic communities, by definition, are groups of scientific and policy experts who share common values and approaches to policy problems regarding specific environmental issues. According to this perspective, the manner in which people and institutions interpret and represent phenomena informs not only the interests of international institutions, but the collective understanding of participants in those institutions as well.[80] Therefore, epistemic communities draw on their technical expertise and skills to elucidate the cause/effect relationship in a specific environmental area and familiarize policy makers with the process of decision-making elsewhere to bring about policy innovation, diffusion, and selection. In this way, epistemic communities can increase the transparency of the international system through the dissemination of knowledge, while creating stable expectations of others behavior by building consensus, and filtering up their agendas for the purpose of encouraging international environmental cooperation.[81] Once again, it seems reasonable to assume that states are more likely to become parties to international environmental treaties that have included the expertise of epistemic communities in the negotiation process.

While the literature on domestic actors portrays both NGOs and epistemic communities as important sources of pressure on states around the world, it must also be recognized that the state often acts autonomously from domestic actors. As Peluso notes, the state often has environmental goals and interests that do not coincide with those of domestic actors: "states generally allocate rights to extract or protect resources in ways that benefit the state itself."[82]

Social Construction of the Environment

According to social construction theorists, the traditional fare of international relations is military and economic considerations. The specific focus on these two dimensions results from the study of international relations being rooted in western modernity. Since environmental issues differ from these two issue areas in both social and physical characteristics, social construction theorists believe a re-examination of the traditional assumptions about actors, perceptions, interests, and relationships is warranted. Accordingly, social construction, or the belief that "social agents produce, reproduce, and redefine the constitutive principles and structures by which and in which they operate,"[83] is one way in which international relations and the international environment may be more easily studied.

According to this view, international politics is understood as a "socially constructed institution that varies across space and time, with multiple meanings and practices that are not set in stone."[84] Environmental problems are believed to be influenced by not only the technological instruments through which information is produced and disseminated, but also by the institutional venue in which problems and solutions are debated and decided.[85] In other words, different people and groups construct their understanding of the global environment and the implications of environmental changes and processes in different ways. This in turn leads to different assumptions and perceptions of environmental needs and different understandings of global ecological interdependence.[86] These competing processes of construction are mediated by a host of social, political and economic institutions.

Three models for the resolution of international environmental problems emerge from the social construction framework. The first model, known as global managerialism, proposes that international environmental solutions not only require strong central protection of environments around the world, but the division of labor between governments and international organizations, with NGOs performing an advisory role on the side. International environmental protection, then, would be best achieved through world conservation and global environmental services. The second model, known as redistributive development, pays greater attention toward equity issues. According to this model, past global inequities and the future of environmentally sound development in the developing world requires the "North" to increase financial and technological assistance to the "South." Finally, the international sustainability model promotes the adoption of global sustainable development practices in the environmental, economic, and social realms to ensure the preservation of the international environment and the continuation of environmentally sound development into the future.[87]

The social constructivist approach, then, attempts to reconcile the incongruities between the political world, delineated by territorial boundaries, and the natural world that is made up of interconnected ecosystems. This approach also permits a more in-depth analysis of international environmental institutions and transnational environmental actors (i.e., NGOs) and the role they play in creating new forms of global governance and authority.[88] While social constructionism does not directly speak to state behavior in regard to international environmental treaties, one might assume, based upon this literature, that the role of local and transnational environmental groups in pressuring states to manage their resources according to internationally agreed upon norms may influence a state's decision to become a party to international environmental treaties—the more pressure from these groups, the more likely a state will become a party to an international environmental treaty. This approach also seems to suggest that the perception of the environmental problem in question may influence state behavior in the international environmental realm—the greater the perception of ecological calamity, the more likely a state will become a party to a specified international environmental treaty.

SUMMARY AND ADDITIONAL CONSIDERATIONS

Various theoretical and practical approaches to international relations and international environmental politics have been presented. Each approach provides a distinct set of assumptions, as well as explanations of state behavior in the international system. The strengths and weakness of each approach have also been identified. Although these approaches provide valuable insights into state behavior, in this author's opinion, the failure of existent literature is the lack of a single comprehensive theory or framework that can address the range of complex processes and factors which have been shown to influence state behavior in the international system and the international environment. Until such a comprehensive framework is constructed, we will be left with singular approaches that only produce partial explanations, limited to a particular area of focus, or a particular level of analysis.

Despite these limitations, the literature review does provide us with valuable insights into state behavior in the international environmental realm. If classical realism accurately describes state behavior, states would be expected to accede to international environmental agreements when it is in their national interest to do so—when an international environmental agreement furthers or does not compromise the national security or power of a given state in the international system. Neorealism, on the other hand, would propose that states are more likely to accede to international environmental treaties when impending environmental degradation threatens the survival of the state or such a treaty does not alter the state's relative power position in the international system. Neoliberalism would propose that state behavior in regard to international environmental treaties would be contingent upon the creation of international regimes and organizations to lower transaction costs and provide monitoring mechanisms. If we look to international law for an explanation of state behavior, we would discover that state behavior is constrained by the costs of deploying new technologies to address such problems and that states are concerned with equity or the fair allocation of costs associated with the implementation and compliance of such treaties. The literature also informs us that it seems reasonable to assume that democracies are more likely to become parties to international environmental agreements than non-democracies. Finally, social constructivism states that the greater the perception of ecological calamity, the more likely a state will accede to a specified international environmental treaty.

As this literature review shows, the means and methods employed at the state level and international level to address international problems associated with environmental degradation have been numerous and wide-ranging. The tremendous complexity of these issues requires a multilevel approach capable of systematically incorporating the numerous partial explanations found in the existing literature. One of the objectives of this book is to propose a new, more comprehensive framework for understanding state behavior in the international environmental realm. This will be accomplished by integrating the above-mentioned explanations provided by various strands of theory and assess the merits of such an approach in an empirical, cross-national manner.

Chapter Three
The History of International Environmentalism

> The history of international environmental action has been of arriving at destinations that looked impossibly distant at the moment of departure.
>
> —Tony Brenton, *The Greening of Machiavelli* (1994)

> The problems that overwhelm us today are precisely those we failed to solve decades ago.
>
> —M.K. Tolba (1982)

In this chapter, I will explore the historical and analytical context of international behavior in the environmental realm. This chapter is divided into six sections. The first section examines the history of international environmentalism prior to the 1960s. The next five sections are devoted to a discussion of relevant events spanning the 1960s to the early 2000s. The final chapter will evaluate the lessons that this historical accounting has to offer. It is my hope that by exploring the history and intellectual context of international environmentalism, we will gain a better understanding of state behavior in this realm and ways to achieve environmental security in the future.

THE PRE-HISTORY OF INTERNATIONAL ENVIRONMENTALISM

Environmental problems and conflicts are hardly a recent global phenomenon. Pollution first arose during ancient times when large numbers of people began living together in cities. In fact, the Romans were one of the first civilizations to document the effects of weather inversions on air pollution in what came to be known as "heavy heaven."[1] Water pollution commonly resulted from the lack of proper sewage systems. More often than not, sewage and other polluting substances were left in the streets or dumped into nearby water supplies. Timbering practices stripped the forests of Greece, Phonecia, and Italy during the rise of classical civilizations. Lead poisoning was common among upper class Romans as they drank lead-sweetened wine and used the remaining grape pulp as a condiment.[2]

These early examples of environmental degradation were localized in their effects. Globalization of environmental degradation can be traced as far back as 1492 with the reciprocal transatlantic invasion of flora and fauna that resulted from Columbus' exploration of the "New World."[3] The creation of sugar cane plantations in South America in the 1600s and the need to increase food supplies in North America, Australia, and Argentina in the 1800s led to massive deforestation of native woods and grasses.[4]

While two of the earliest texts on international law and pollution emerged in the late 17th century,[5] it was not until the advent of the Industrial Revolution in the 1700s and early 1800s that environmental degradation became a serious problem with widespread implications. Some of the more notable examples of the effects of industrialization include: 1) the disruption of the flow of every stream in France by the 100,000 mills located there; 2) the indiscriminate dumping of waste in local water supplies spawning a far reaching cholera epidemic throughout Europe in the 1830s; and, 3) high levels of air pollution which caused respiratory diseases that affected millions of individuals around the world as early as the 1870s. While some states embarked on bilateral programs to deal with the side effects of environmental degradation, it was not until the middle of the 19th century and early 20th century that multilateral attempts to address these concerns were initiated.

During the middle of the 19th century, many states recognized that the effects of a number of environmental problems had international ramifications—what one state did within its borders could have a material impact on other states. The first attempts to form multilateral environmental agreements followed this realization. With Western Europe and the United States already tackling particular conservation and pollution issues during this time, it is no surprise that it was also these states that advanced the idea of global environmental management. International commissions were set up in the mid-19th century to govern such bodies of water as the Rhine and the Danube Rivers. In 1872, the Swiss proposed the establishment of an international commission to protect migrating birds. In 1900, the *Convention for the Preservation of Animals, Birds, and Fish in Africa* was signed in London by the European colonial powers with the intention of preserving game in east Africa by limiting ivory exports.[6]

While these initial agreements tended to be regional in scope, the late 19th century and early 20th century saw the emergence of environmental agreements with a larger geographical magnitude. The convention to protect fur seals, the agreement among littoral states on the management of the Rhine, and the protection of the spawning grounds of North Atlantic salmon are three such examples of these more expansive treaties. The first attempt at truly global environmental management dates back to 1909 when the United States undertook efforts to convene a world conference on natural resource conservation.

International organizations, created during this time, assumed environmental responsibilities during the first half of the 20th century. The Food and Agricultural Organization (FAO) took on the responsibility for the conservation of natural resources. The International Labour Organization (ILO) assumed responsibility for the protection of workers against occupational environmental hazards. Finally, the International Maritime Organization (IMO) oversaw marine pollution control.

During the interwar years (1920s–1930s), environmental concerns took on greater international dimensions. The League of Nations attempted to address marine pollution issues, but efforts to bring about a treaty on the control of marine pollution caused by ships failed to receive adequate international support to become binding. Despite the failure to reach international consensus, this was the first time that the international community negotiated an environmental agreement with global implications. A later negotiation involving whaling, which led to the adoption of a whaling convention in 1931,[7] appears to be the first global resource management or conservation instrument formally recognized by the international community.

The first international inquiry into air pollution damage, and subsequent international resolution of this issue, also took place during this time period. In the 1930s, the Rocky Mountain's Columbia River Valley (located in the United States) suffered extensive vegetation and farm crop damage. An international investigation was launched to determine the source of the destruction. A smelter in British Columbia, Canada was eventually identified as the source of the emissions responsible for the loss of vegetation and crops and Canada was ordered by the international community to compensate the United States for damages in the "Trial Smelter" case (1935).

Throughout much of the 1940s, the international community was preoccupied by the demands of carrying out a world war. Despite these demands, states in the international system were able to forge a number of international agreements on conservation by the end of World War II. These treaties, for the most part, focused on the protection of migratory birds and wildlife.

Unfortunately, sparse ratification and poor adherence to the terms of these treaties contributed to their overall ineffectiveness.[8]

The technological advancements of World War II contributed to tremendous economic growth in the 1950s. Environmental considerations took a back seat to economic development because the two were often viewed as incompatible.[9] Although there was little international environmental law produced during the 1950s, the first international instrument to tackle pollution (rather than conservation) emerged in 1954: *The International Convention for the Prevention of Oil Pollution.*[10]

THE RISE OF INTERNATIONAL ENVIRONMENTALISM: THE 1960S

International environmentalism in the 1960s is characterized as a period in which an upsurge in public concern over the state of the environment led to environmental issues being incorporated into the international political agenda. What brought about this dramatic change in public and international attitudes toward the environment?

One event, which is often identified as marking the birth of new environmental consciousness, was a book written about the dangers of toxic chemicals. An indictment on the excessive use of pesticides, *Silent Spring,* written by Rachel Carson in 1962, forced individuals and governments to examine the public health and environmental implications of using chemicals to stimulate food production.[11]

Ecological calamities also played a role in intensifying public concern over the state of the environment. Incidents such as the Torrey canyon oil spill (1967) off the coast of England and the oil well explosion in California's Santa Barbara Channel (1969) "initiated disaster-driven international agreements."[12] The Torrey Canyon accident was the largest oil spill to date and the intensity of public pressure generated as a result of this accident brought about the negotiation of three treaties by the international community to address: 1) the allocation of rights to act in such cases; 2) the toughening of state liability and compensation arrangements; and, 3) the creation of an international fund to provide such compensation. Soon after the Torrey Canyon incident, a series of regional oil pollution treaties were established for the North Sea, North East Atlantic and Scandinavian states.[13] Moreover, public and international concerns regarding the irreversible effects of aboveground nuclear testing led to the negotiation and adoption of the Limited Test Ban Treaty in 1963.

International environmental issues were slowly becoming a regular part of the United Nations (UN) agenda. In 1962, the UN produced the *Declaration of the UN Commission on Permanent Sovereignty Over Natural Resources* that guaranteed the "rights of peoples and nations to sovereignty over their natural wealth and resources."[14] In 1967, the United Nations Education, Scientific, and Cultural Organization (UNESCO), with support from a number of other UN bodies, convened the *Intergovernmental Conference of Experts to Consider the Scientific Basis for the Rational Use and the Conservation of the Resources of the Biosphere.*[15] In 1968, the United Nations General Assembly (UNGA) called for an international conference to examine "the problems of the human environment and also to identify those aspects of it that can only, or best be solved through international cooperation and agreement."[16] The purpose of the conference, to be held in Stockholm in 1972, was to

> provide a framework for comprehensive consideration within the UN of the problems of the human environment in order to focus the attention of the governments and public opinion on the importance and urgency of this question.[17]

In sum, various factors and events in the 1960s influenced growing public and international concern for the environment. First, there was not only an increase in the levels of pollution, but a greater number of environmental catastrophes than in previous years. Second, there was greater attention focused on environmental issues in the media, especially the Western press. Third, growing levels of material affluence in the developed economies of the 1960s produced a shift in preferences from increased material consumption to improvements in the non-material factors of life such as environmental quality.[18] This shift in attitude toward the environment was accompanied by a tremendous growth in membership of existing nature groups and the formation of new environmental groups.[19] Finally, emerging environmental issues were not only intrinsically international in nature—oceans, migratory species and global atmosphere—they brought about increased public awareness of events outside one's own national borders and increased public attention to issues of international scope of which the environment was a prominent example. Despite this growing awareness, perceptions of and responses to environmental degradation varied across states in the 1960s.

STOCKHOLM AND THE INTERNATIONAL ENVIRONMENT: THE 1970S

The 1970s have been identified as the starting point for the modern study of international environmental regulation and of the international environmental movement. In addition to the plethora of public and international activity that occurred during this time period,[20] it was not until the *United Nations Conference on the Human Environment (1972),* that growing international concerns regarding the impact of environmental degradation on the human population and the international ramifications of the depletion of finite resources were first voiced. As a result of the Stockholm Conference, the international community recognized the collective responsibility of all states for the preservation of the earth and its biosphere.

The Intellectual and Scientific Debate Over the State of the Environment

At the start of the 1970s, not only did environmental issues take on increasing importance in the international arena, they became a major focus of research and debate within the academic and scientific communities. In 1971, Harold and Margaret Sprouts published their seminal book, *Toward A Politics of Planet Earth*. This work represents one of the earliest efforts to make environmental thinking the epistemological basis for a theory of international relations. Furthermore, it is one of the first analyses to suggest global governance as an appropriate response to international environmental threats.[21]

At the same time, the intellectual and scientific communities were engaged in debate over the prospects for environmental sustainability into the future. Early works by Paul Ehrlich (*The Population Bomb*, 1970) and Barry Commoner (*The Closing Circle*, 1971) argued that human prospects of survival were seriously endangered by global environmental degradation. These findings were supported by the work of the *Club of Rome*. Using computer-generated models, a group of seventy eminent scientists, economists, and businessmen concluded that without limits to growth, the earth was headed for an environmental apocalypse.[22] According to the "limits to growth" perspective, the exponential nature of population growth and subsequent demands placed on the environment by a growing population would deplete the supply of finite resources. Given the interplay of resource use, decay of renewable resources (such as air, water, and soil), food supply, and population density, industrial civilization was not sustainable.[23]

Other mainstream academia and members of industry questioned the catastrophic nature of environmental destruction that had been forecasted. John Maddox, in his book *The Doomsday Syndrome* (1972), described the *Club of Rome's* findings as an "overreaction to some of the supposed dangers of environmental contamination."[24] Others argued that increased political concern over the long-term impact of environmental degradation was grotesquely out of proportion to its true importance, in part due to melodramatic media coverage.[25]

Questions regarding the strategy of limiting growth in order to ensure environmental protection became the focus of debate between the developed and developing states. The resulting "North-South" divide deserves to be mentioned here because it not only illustrates the existing tensions between the perceptions of the role of environment and development, the disparity in attitudes regarding the environment and development became the basis of negotiations between states at the Stockholm Conference in 1972.

According to the developing countries, limiting or cutting off their growth-based economies would deny poorer countries any prospect of escaping the poverty trap. Many of the more serious environmental problems faced by the South were the result of extreme poverty and lack of social and economic development. Since the problem in the developing world appeared to be too little industry by which to stimulate necessary economic and social growth, some pollution seemed to be worth the price of increasing the overall living standard in these countries. Because the North had defined global environmental issues solely in terms of pollution abatement and as technical problems, the South believed that limiting growth might be a tactic of the rich countries to keep the poor countries from industrializing. Furthermore, developing countries were concerned that future development would be impacted if Northern financial aid were diverted toward environmental protection problems.

These concerns were formalized in a meeting of scientists and experts from the developing world at Founex, Switzerland in 1971. The *Founex Report* stated that international concern for the environment stemmed from the pollution and disruption of natural systems caused by high levels of industrialization. Therefore, according to the developing countries, industrialized countries were responsible for much of the environmental degradation currently under international scrutiny. The central environmental problems facing developing countries stemmed not from pollution but from poverty, disease, hunger, and exposure to natural disasters. Therefore, the solution was continued economic development, not pollution abatement or "limits to growth" strategies. In conclusion, the South was afraid that Northern concern regarding environmental damage that resulted from industrialization would create pressures to slow down industrial growth worldwide including the developing world. The South would therefore emphasize sovereignty or the rights of countries to choose their own path of economic development, free from international interference for environmental and other reasons. This platform would become the basis of the developing world's agenda in negotiations at the *United Nations Conference on the Human Environment (1972)*.

The Road to Stockholm

As mentioned previously, in 1968, the United Nations General Assembly called for an international conference to examine the problems of the human environment. The *United Nations Conference on the Human Environment (UNCHE)* was scheduled to take place in Stockholm in 1972. Preparation for the conference took place between 1970–1972. United Nations member states and component parts of the UN were invited to participate in the conference. Each state was expected to prepare a comprehensive report on its environmental situation and the policies it was putting into place to address environmental concerns. One hundred and ten such reports were received prior to the start of the conference.

The United Nations Conference on the Human Environment, Stockholm 1972

The *United Nations Conference on the Human Environment* provided a forum through which the international community could address its global environmental concerns. Not only was this the first "theme" conference sponsored by the United Nations, it was the first international environmental summit ever held. One hundred and fourteen nations participated in the conference. Two distinctive features of UNCHE became highly characteristic of future international environmental conferences: 1) the extent of media coverage; and, 2) the substantial involvement of non-governmental organizations (NGOs).

NGOs had become an active force in western environmental policymaking during the 1960s. At the urging of western states, conference organizers gave NGOs a major role not only during the preparatory process, but also through out the conference. Three organized environmental forums for NGOs took place outside the official proceedings of Stockholm: The Environment Forum, the People's Forum, and the Dai Dong. The purpose of these gatherings was to provide a setting in which NGOs could debate various environmental proposals and make presentations. In addition to the forums, NGOs were permitted to make formal statements to the conference. Over all, five hundred NGOs participated in the Stockholm proceedings. As a result of both media coverage and NGO participation, the negotiation of international texts became a more open process than had previously been the case.

Despite the above-mentioned characteristics of UNCHE, it was the range of perceptions and priorities among states that defined this international event. The growing intensity of western public concern and events surrounding Earth Day in the United States, led western countries in the United Nations General Assembly to strengthen the formal aims of the conference from mere conscious raising to a more action oriented process. However, western enthusiasm was not shared elsewhere in the world.

The communist bloc argued that pollution was the product of capitalism and a problem they did not suffer from. Furthermore, Cold War tensions surrounding the international status of East Germany prompted the Soviet Union and East European nations to bow out of the preparatory process and conference itself—UNCHE was not considered a high political priority among the communist countries.

The developing countries approached the conference with caution, using the *Founex Report* (1971) as the basis of their platform. While the developed North wanted to draw attention to marine pollution, the over consumption of natural resources, and global population growth, the South insisted the conference's agenda be broadened to include such issues as global poverty and foreign aid levels. The South not only argued that their principle need was for economic growth, even if pollution and over consumption of natural resources were part of this development, they justified their request for increased foreign aid by insisting the North should compensate them for the costs of meeting higher environmental standards. This assistance should supplement existing aid flows. Surprised by the South's approach, the North, in particular the United States, remained steadfast in their opposition to principles of compensation and additionality.

In addition to differences of opinion over foreign aid and general perceptions of the relationship between the environment and development, specific environmental issues became the objects of discontent within the international community. Pressure from the Swedish delegation to adopt strong measures against acid rain met resistance from those developed countries where acid rain originated. Rather than a pro-active agreement on acid rain, the disputing parties settled on a recommendation that called for further monitoring of the problem. International concern over continuing deforestation was undermined by Brazil's insistence that it had sovereignty over its natural resources, including forests. Debates surrounding atmospheric nuclear testing pitted the United States and New Zealand against France and China. Divisions over marine protection created a rift between states who wanted to give coastal states greater authority over activities in their neighboring waters and states that had substantial marine interests and wanted to maintain the freedom of the seas. With the support of other countries, that just so happened to reverse their initial positions of support after the conference, the *International Whaling Commission* killed an agreement proposed by the United States and various non-governmental organizations that imposed a ten-year moratorium on whaling.

The conference did produce three noteworthy texts: 1) the *Declaration on the Human Environment*; 2) an *Action Plan for the Human Environment*;

and, 3) the Resolution on Institutional and Financial Arrangements. The Declaration on the Human Environment, also known as the "Stockholm Declaration," consisted of twenty-six principles. Intended to provide the groundwork for future development, the "Stockholm Declaration" tried to ease North-South tensions by laying the foundation for future international environmental law making while balancing the call for natural resource conservation and pollution reduction with the need for economic development.[26] Specifically, *Principle 21* dealt not only with the rights of states to exploit their own resources in line with their own environmental policies, it addressed a state's responsibility to ensure that activities in their control did not cause damage to the environment of other states.

The *Action Plan for the Human Environment* consisted of 109 recommendations for governmental and intergovernmental action across the environmental spectrum. However, one of the significant problems with the Action Plan was it only provided recommendations and not binding agreements. Consequently, states and multilateral organizations could decide for themselves how far they would implement them, if they implemented them at all. Although the document does provide a number of recommendations for international environmental treaties, these recommendations simply provided encouragement for matters that were already underway or planned.[27]

In an attempt to find appropriate funding mechanisms for international environmental activities, a resolution to create a new UN environmental body and funding agency was agreed upon by conference participants—the *United Nations Environmental Programme (UNEP).* Although a number of UN agencies with environmental responsibilities[28] were already in existence, it was apparent to many states, especially those in the developed world, that the international system could benefit from a central agency whose main focus was for environmental activities and that would act as a means to coordinate activities of various agencies and states. It was hoped that UNEP would be able to prod the UN system and governments of the world into more sound environmental management. Maurice Strong, Secretary General of the Stockholm Conference, found a way to manage conflicting North-South interests by recommending that UNEP and the "Environmental Fund" it would administer be set up within the existing UN structure and that a large governing council be created to ensure an equal voice to the developing countries.

The Lessons of Stockholm

According to Tony Brenton, the formal products of the *United Nations Conference on the Human Environment* have only had a marginal effect on the subsequent history of international environmental action. The *"Stockholm Declaration"* did not become the guiding force for international law that it was intended to be and the *Action Plan* did little more than catalogue existing environmental concerns and activities rather than direct them or push them forward.[29] According to UNEP, ten years after Stockholm, the *Action Plan* had only been partially implemented and with unsatisfactory results. While some progress was made in the areas of monitoring, information exchange, research, and consciousness raising (all of which are relatively inexpensive), little headway was made in areas that cut across economic or developmental interests or that required major changes of policy and administration.

In its early years, the principal role of UNEP was to raise global environmental consciousness and collaborate with other agencies. However, lack of funding from the international community combined with its peripheral geographical location,[30] diluted any influence the agency might have had. As Eckholm notes, UNEP was not a powerful source of change, "for when their immediate economic and political interests are affected, national governments have proved unwilling to grant significant powers to an international authority."[31]

Some scholars have described the *United Nations Conference on the Human Environment* as merely a cosmetic event because: 1) its conclusions were vacuous and rarely implemented; 2) the institutional arrangements and financial commitments were marginal; and, 3) international environmental law remained underdeveloped. However, one should not be so quick to overlook the lasting contributions this conference made to international environmentalism. First, the *Stockholm Conference* recognized growing western public and governmental concern for environmental issues. Second, it exposed the gulf between developed and developing countries' perceptions and priorities, and the impossibility of discussing and resolving environmental issues without also facing the developmental issues linked to them. Furthermore, the conference increased awareness that environmental deterioration and the depletion of natural resources led to a cycle of poverty in many areas of the world. Fourth, international environmental diplomacy was conducted largely in the open with intense media and NGO attention. Finally, UNCHE had an overwhelming influence on international relations. Not only did Stockholm redefine international issues to include natural resources, pollution, conflict and balance between development and the environment; it redefined the rationale behind cooperation to include common interests in the preservation of the biosphere. It also promoted a new attitude toward international responsibility, whereby the developed world was obliged (at least on paper) to assist the developing nations in reconciling their developmental efforts with environmental quality objectives.[32] These efforts led to a new understanding of rights and obligations among developed and developing nations.[33] As Lynton Caldwell notes, "the Stockholm Conference is a major landmark in the effort of nations to collectively protect their life-support base on earth."[34]

The Post-Stockholm Era: International Environmental Developments 1973–1979

Immediately after UNCHE, there was an increase in the volume of international environmental business. The *Regional Seas Program* took hold with the adoption of the North Sea and Mediterranean Sea conventions. The UNEP Governing Council pressed member states to ratify four of the major conventions negotiated during or immediately after Stockholm: 1) the *World Heritage Convention* 11/23/72; 2) the *London Dumping Convention 12/29/72;* 3) *the Convention on International Trade in Endangered Species (CITES) 3/3/73;*[35] and, 4) *International Convention on the Prevention of Pollution from Ships* (MARPOL) 11/2/73. However, states did not appear in a hurry to act when these international environmental treaties were opened for ratification. It was the relatively low priority given these specific treaties rather than domestic opposition that impeded the ratification process.[36] Consequently, post-Stockholm efforts to extend international environmental law by conventional methods were slow to yield positive results. Environmental activity became dependent on political pressure from individual states rather than on any agreement or machinery that the Stockholm conference created.

In the developed North, UNCHE represented a high point in public and governmental attention to the environment. Governmental action throughout the 1970s resolved some of the more immediate environmental problems. European countries tackled the problem of acid rain despite the large clean up costs involved. The European Community (EC) launched joint environmental legislation and made environmental protection one of its priorities. Environmental spending in the North increased from 1% to 2% of the Gross National Product.[37] As Brenton noted, governmental activity in the North was "an impressive demonstration of the ability of these polities to respond to environmental problems at the national level when motivated to do so."[38] Part of the North's success in dealing with environmental issues resulted from the gradually shifting away from setting emission limits for pollutants to more market oriented techniques, which had the advantage of achieving the same environmental objectives in a more economically efficient way. However, it is also important to note that there was also a significant shift in the amount of heavy polluting industry away from the North to the developing world as a result of tighter regulations in the North.

While the intensity of western public concern regarding the environment rocketed in 1960s, it began to diminish in the second half of the 1970s. It was not that public concern disappeared altogether or reverted back to pre-1960s levels, but rather, reflected: 1) the public's increasing familiarity with environmental issues; 2) less media coverage of environmental issues; or, 3) the emergence of other significant issues such as the oil shocks and economic slowdown of the early 1970s.

At the same time, the South was experiencing an intensification of environmental problems. Having identified poverty and population growth, and economic growth and industrialization as the two most serious problems facing the developing world, UNEP and the *United Nations Commission on Trade and Development (UNCTAD)*[39] organized the *Cocoyoc Symposium* in 1974 to examine the development and environmental concerns voiced by developing nations at UNCHE two years earlier.

The symposium concluded that economic and social factors were often the root cause of environmental degradation in the developing world. Since states placed different demands on the earth's biosphere, the richer countries were able to preempt and waste many of the cheap available resources while leaving poorer countries few options but to destroy readily available natural resources. Rather than follow in the footsteps of the industrialized world, countries in the developing world would have to rely on their own developmental models to achieve higher living standards. The primary goal of the international community, according to countries in the South, should be to find ways that meet not only the basic needs of the world's population, but also the needs of the poorest segment of humanity without jeopardizing the plant's carrying capacity. The *Cocoyoc Symposium* reinforced the call for international action to deal with acute problems of poverty in the developing countries, as well as lay the foundations for sustainable development.

Unlike the North, increasing environmental stresses in the developing world were not accompanied by the growth of environmental movements. On the one hand, authoritarian regimes in the developing world have been known to limit participation in and the activities of social movements. On the other hand, there is a lack of tradition in grass roots political activism that hamper the evolution of such movements. Where environmental movements did emerge, they did so in countries on the way toward industrialization.

Despite widespread popular indifference, many governments in the South began developing environmental policies consistent with their national self-interest.[40] Worldwide, ministerial-level departments of the environment rose from fewer than ten in 1970 to over one hundred in 1994, the majority of which were located in the developing world.[41] New legislation was introduced covering environmental issues such as the protection of water, forests, wildlife, soils, coasts, natural resources and sanitation. In the developing countries, where popular interest in the environment was sporadic and local in its focus,[42] environmental policy was a top-down process, whereby national governments became the driving force behind policy development.[43] While governments in the South established agencies and laws to address environmental concerns, popular pressures and enforcement mechanisms were not yet adequate to reverse the growing tide of pollution.

International Environmental Issues of Significance: The 1970s

The number of international environmental agreements reached during the 1960s was double that for the 1950s. The number of environmental agreements more than doubled again in the 1970s. Most of these international environmental treaties were devoted to marine pollution,[44] so by the time of UNCHE, there were already several conventions on the pollution of oceans especially by oil. The International Maritime Organization *(IMO)* had a well-developed infrastructure and a long track record of organizing marine pollution negotiations.[45] The Stockholm recommendations proposed the extension of the marine pollution regime. First, the global application of the *Oslo Convention*, which controls the dumping of wastes in the North Sea, quickly evolved into the *London Dumping Convention* (1972). Secondly, continuation of the work associated with the *International Convention on Oil Pollution* (1954), which had already been strengthened numerous times, was done in 1973 with the negotiation of the *International Convention on the Prevention of Pollution from Ships (MARPOL)*.[46] Signatories of MARPOL tended to be states with long coastlines and shipping industries small enough to be undeterred by costs. However, the MARPOL provisions were so wideranging and costly that states with large tanker fleets were slow to ratify it.[47] Since UNCHE, the international community has primarily focused on regional conventions regarding the seas and oceans rather than global treaties.

The international community has a long track record of international agreements concerning the conservation of plants and animals. Traditionally, international activity in this area has been driven more by western public affection for wildlife than any real assessment of the value and costs of its preservation. Huge rates of growth in the trade of animal species during the 1950s and 1960s elicited calls for global regulation. In 1973, the international community negotiated the *Convention on International Trade in Endangered Species of Flora and Fauna* (CITES).

This convention imposed a ban on trade in over six hundred species and required controls on trade in over 26,000 others. Furthermore, trade with non-parties to this treaty was also banned unless the non-parties had introduced CITES like controls. CITES is considered one of the most successful international wildlife conservation treaties for several reasons. First, amendments to the treaty have strengthened the self-interest of parties by promoting ranching and allowing endangered species to be bred for use and trade—protection is achieved through financial self-interest. Second, the administrative system established for CITES was a departure from traditional environmental institution building. A permanent secretariat was established to provide oversight to the treaty. All parties to the treaty were required to set up agencies to enforce the terms of the convention. Parties to the convention were expected to communicate on a regular basis with each other and the secretariat. Finally, regular meetings of the parties were to be held to review the implementation of convention and create opportunities for international and public pressure to bring about change.

Three additional global negotiations of significance were held during the 1970s: 1) *The UN Conference on the Law of the Sea (UNCLOS)*, 1973–1982; 2) *New International Economic Order (NIEO)*; and, 3) *UN Conference on Desertification (UNCOD)* 1977. Unlike other negotiations carried out at during the 1970s, these three negotiations ended unsuccessfully, due in part to the divergence in North-South agendas.

The *UN Conference on the Law of the Sea* lasted from 1973 to 1982. The purpose of the conference was to examine the full scope of marine related topics, especially those related to the environment. However, tensions between the North and South led to a stalemate until 1994, when the sixty countries necessary for it to enter into force ratified the treaty.

In the early 1970s, developing countries demanded that world trade and industry be restructured in their favor. The *New International Economic Order (NIEO)*, as this strategy was known, advocated: 1) increased foreign aid from the developed world and multilateral lending agencies; 2) freer access to markets in the North; 3) commodity agreements to stabilize the prices of raw materials and primary products upon which these countries depend; and, 4) international controls over foreign investment and international management of projects to develop the wealth on the world's sea beds.[48] While essentially a developmental policy, because it sought the redistribution of wealth and economic power in favor of developing countries, this process had considerable environmental overtones. But by the end of the 1970s, the NIEO had come to a dead end. The negotiations finally collapsed at the *Cancun Summit* in 1981.

The *United Nations Conference on Desertification (UNCOD)* was held in Nairobi, Kenya in 1977. This conference was promoted by developing countries threatened by the process of desertification. A plan of action to tackle the problem of desertification was produced. However, the incorporation of a voluntary funding mechanism meant few states would provide the necessary financial assistance to implement the agreement.

Summary of the 1970s

The modern study of international environmentalism began in the 1970s. Throughout the decade, academia and scientists were engaged in a series of debates regarding the long-term implications of global environmental degradation. In the midst of these debates, the international community recognized their collective responsibility for environmental preservation and came together at Stockholm in 1972 to examine the human environment and find solutions to a myriad of environmental problems. Although the international community was able to successfully negotiate a series of international environmental treaties,[49] other issues remained unresolved.[50] Despite some failures, there was an overall increase in the volume of international environmental business. In fact, of the 170 international environmental treaties adopted, over two-thirds of these treaties were adopted since Stockholm in 1972.[51]

Environmental protection became the focus of debate between the developed North and developing South. The disparity in perceptions and attitudes regarding the environment and development came to define international environmental activity of the 1970s. Lack of social and economic development were the root cause of environmental decline in the South, therefore, some pollution would be worth the price of economic growth and the overall increase of living standards in the developing world. In order to cooperate in the international environmental arena, the North should be willing to provide increased aid and technology to offset the additional burdens of conforming to environmental standards. However, the North in general has resisted such requests. As will be discussed through out the remainder of this text, very little has changed in regard to this debate.

THE 1980S: SECOND COMING OF INTERNATIONAL ENVIRONMENTALISM

Through out the 1980s, there was a rebirth in international and public concern regarding the environment. However, where international concern had been previously focused on issues of resource management, issues related to pollution now took center stage. Climatic and other environmental disasters,[52] growing scientific knowledge, strong economic growth and prosperity in the industrialized world, and the release of the Bruntland report brought global environmental issues to the top of the international political agenda by the late 1980s. Furthermore, the United Nations and United Nations Environmental Programme initiated much of the significant international environmental activity that occurred in regard to these issues.

The United Nations and the World Environment

In May 1982, at the tenth anniversary session of the Stockholm Conference, the United Nations reviewed the extent to which the UNCHE Action Plan had been implemented. The UN noted that while general environmental trends did not appear as cataclysmic as they once did, many forms of degradation were shown to have long-term implications. If environmental problems were to be resolved, extensive behavioral modification was required. Although outlining the appropriate responses to environmental degradation was difficult, generating the political will to endorse and comply with such measures was worse. As discussed in the *World Charter for Nature,* adopted by the UN General Assembly in October 1982,[53] making environmental principles operational in a world of sovereign states made the formulation of international environmental policy difficult.

The task of the World Commission on Environment and Development (WCED), set up as an independent body in 1983 by the UNGA, was to re-examine critical environmental and developmental problems and to formulate realistic proposals to solve them. The WCED (also known as the Brundtland Commission) met formally for the first time in October 1984, and in 1987, they published their findings in Our Common Future. One of the lasting contributions of *Our Common Future* was to link environmental protection to the issue of global economic growth and development through the use of sustainable development.[54] Therefore, the primary goal of all economic sectors should be conservation rather than development alone. Furthermore, any new era of economic growth must assure that poorer nations receive their fair share of the necessary resources required for sustained growth. The Brundtland Commission was able to amass greater knowledge and understanding of the impact of continued environmental degradation. It also recognized that while multilateral solutions to environmental problems would require global management strategies, national security concerns and state sovereignty were likely to impede any such move toward global governance.

In 1988, the UNGA accepted the recommendations of the WECD and called for another environmental summit. In 1989, the actual details of the conference were hammered out between the member states of the United Nations. The *United Nations Conference on the Environment and Development* (also known as the Earth Summit) was to be held in Rio de Janeiro, Brazil in June 1992. The most difficult issues arising in those preliminary negotiations concerned foreign aid and technology transfers. The objective of UNCED would be to identify ways to provide new and additional financial resources and provide favorable access to and transfer of technology. At the same time that states were discussing the details of the conference, the United Nations launched a global negotiation on climate change while UNEP launched a similar negotiation involving biodiversity. Both the United Nations and UNEP hoped to have the treaties ready for signature at UNCED.

Additional support for increased international environmental action came from the *Hague Declaration* (1989). The declaration called for: 1) new environmental institutions; 2) the expansion of UN authority to deal with global environmental problems; and, 3) the International Court of Justice (ICJ) to impose its jurisdiction over the implementation of UN environmental treaties. The absence of the United States, China, Great Britain and the former Soviet Union from the proceedings ensured the declaration would have little international momentum.

The Growing Status of UNEP

The United Nations Environmental Programme became increasingly important in the 1980s. In its infancy, UNEP had little influence over states in the international system. Nor did it have much influence in persuading international lending institutions to incorporate environmental considerations into their lending programs. In 1980, UNEP, the United Nations Developmental Programme (UNDP), the World Bank, and several regional developmental institutions promised to incorporate environmental matters in developmental policy. They also agreed to increase collaboration in the future.

In collaboration with UNEP, the International Union for the Conservation of Nature and Natural Resources (IUCN) and the World Wildlife Federation (WWF) published the World Conservation Strategy in 1980. This document brought about a turning point in international thinking about economic development and the protection of the biosphere by suggesting that ecological sustainable development was the key to economic progress. Moreover, it identified three objectives for the conservation of living resources: 1) maintenance of essential ecological processes and life-support systems; 2) the preservation of biological diversity; and, 3) the sustainable use of species and ecosystems. It also suggested that environmental policies should anticipate environmental degradation rather than react and attempt to cure it. Finally, from an international perspective, the *World Conservation Strategy* advocated the protection of the global commons: atmosphere, oceans and continent of Antarctica. While comprehensive in its presentation, the weakness of the document was the lack of provisions promoting the strategy and for monitoring its progress.

By 1981, environmental law and sound development had become increasingly important to countries through out the world. Since numerous environmental treaties, guidelines, and principles had already been developed under the auspices of UNEP, the Governing Council convened an ad hoc meeting of senior government officials in Montevideo, Uruguay (1981). The purpose of this meeting was to establish a framework, methods, and program for development and periodic review of international, regional, and national environmental law. The *Montevideo Process* identified the following areas as deserving international action: environmental emergencies; coastal zone management; soil conservation; transboundary air pollution; international trade in potentially harmful chemicals; protection from pollution of inland waterways; legal and administrative mechanisms for the prevention and redress of pollution damage; and, methods of environmental impact assessment. Many conventions covering these specified areas became binding after Montevideo: the *Vienna Convention for the Protection of the Ozone Layer and Montreal Protocol; the Zambezi River and Lake Chad Basin Action Plans and Legal Instruments;* Regional Seas conventions and protocols; the *Basel Convention on the Control of Transboundary Movement of Hazardous Wastes and Their Disposal;* and, regional agreements on land-based sources of marine pollution. Since Montevideo, threats to biodiversity and the implications of climate change and global warming have been added to the above named list.

At the 1982 *Session of Special Character,* the General Council of UNEP reviewed the major achievements in the implementation of the UNCHE Action Plan adopted at Stockholm.[55] In regard to environmental assessment, the General Council found that although the Global Environmental Monitoring System (GEMS) was operative there were gaps in development, coordination, and user applications. International studies of climate change undertaken by the Global Atmospheric Research Program (GARP) had been incorporated into the World Climate Program. The International Referral System for Sources of Environmental Information (IRSSEI) had not fully realized its objectives due to slow growth in user demand. The *International Registry of*

Potentially Toxic Chemicals (IRPTC) had become an important center for information. Finally, the International Program on Chemical Safety (IPCS) was providing toxicological assessments for an increased number of substances. In addition to these findings, the UNEP Governing Council called for two reports on the environment and development in 1983, which resulted in the publication of Our Common Future (1987) and the UNEP Environmental Perspective to the Year 2000 and beyond. Finally, in 1988, the General Council of UNEP adopted the System-wide Medium Term Environmental Program for 1990-1995 as an important mechanism for the coordination of environmental activities within the UN system.

INTERNATIONAL ENVIRONMENTAL ISSUES OF SIGNIFICANCE: THE 1980S

Although the 1980s saw a slight decline in the overall number of international environmental agreements reached from the 1970 level, there was triple the number of agreements reached during the 1950s. Furthermore there was significant growth in the number of regional treaties, with only a small minority of regional agreements negotiated in the 1950s and 1960s, to two-thirds of all major environmental treaties negotiated in the 1980s.

The *United Nations Conference on New and Renewable Sources of Energy (UNCNRSE)* was held in Nairobi in 1981. The North-South divide was ever present at the conference. States agreed upon an action plan, but the conference failed to produce the mechanisms necessary for the implementation of the plan.

Table 3.1 International Environmental Treaties, 1920–2000: Classified by Geographical Scope and Environmental Treaty Type

	Regional		Global	
	Resource Management	Pollution Control	Resource Management	Pollution Control
1920s	0	0	0	1
1930s	0	0	1	0
1940s	2	0	2	0
1950s	8	0	6	1
1960s	7	3	6	11
1970s	14	13	8	16
1980s	13	21	4	12
1990-2000	7	5	4	6

Despite public pressure to address nuclear issues, very little was accomplished by the international community. Environmental issues associated with nuclear technology were not discussed at the Stockholm Conference in 1972. The developed countries kept the discussion of nuclear issues off the agenda of the UNCNRSE held in 1981. When the issue did find its way onto the international agenda, countries with no nuclear industry tried to use the international system to impose tougher standards on countries with nuclear capabilities. For a long time, the only real international work on nuclear issues was highly technical, such as agreements reached in 1962 and 1971 on liability in the event of a radiation accident. It was not until the explosion of the Chernobyl nuclear power plant in 1986, that this pattern would change. Immediately following this nuclear disaster, two international environmental conventions of global importance were negotiated: the *Early Notification of Nuclear Accident (1986) and Assistance in Case of Nuclear Accident* (1986).

Mounting evidence of western states dumping their toxic wastes in Africa, led to the negotiation of the *Basel Convention on the Transboundary Movement of Hazardous Waste* in 1989. This was the first international negotiation where developing countries, led by Africa, were demanding tougher environmental regulation than the West.

Motivated by western public concern and conflicting territorial claims,[56] the international community erected a framework for the environmental protection of Antarctica that would allow them to keep their options open for the possibility of exploiting vast mineral and oil reserves in the future. In 1988, the *Convention on the Regulation of Antarctic Mineral Resource Activities (CRAMA)* was denounced as a mining charter by NGOs, and, in 1990, Australia and France rejected the convention out right and proposed Antarctica be designated as a world park. Finally, in 1991, CRAMA was replaced by a fifty-year moratorium on all mineral related activity.

Conventions concerning atmospheric pollution were not well established prior to Stockholm. In fact, the Stockholm principles contained little reference to the problem because governments did not generally acknowledge atmospheric pollution as an international problem. International opinion would change with the discovery of an ozone hole over Antarctica. This discovery led to the negotiation of the *Vienna Convention on the Protection of the Ozone Layer* (1985), and it subsequent protocols: the *Montreal Protocol on Substances that Deplete the Ozone Layer* (1987) and the *London Protocol* (1990). These particular negotiations exemplified many of the key features of modern international environmental business. First, pressure to reach an appropriate resolution was generated in both the political and popular spheres. Secondly, industries that would be most affected by any change in policy played an important role in the negotiation process. Third, Southern cooperation was contingent on Northern financial and technological help. Finally, the negotiations had an important institutional dimension whereby UNEP played key role in the negotiation process and a new institutional structure with regular meetings of experts, officials and ministers; a permanent secretariat; arrangements for information and data exchange; and, an international fund was erected.

Although the international community had been successful in its attempts to tackle problems of hazardous waste and ozone depletion, it did less well resolving issues involving tropical forests. Contrary to popular thought, the developing countries, home to the majority of tropical forests, were resistant to international efforts to halt deforestation. In fact, many developing countries, most notably Brazil, encouraged deforestation as part of their economic development strategy. Given that the North had material interests in the tropical forests,[57] it seemed odd that the concentration of concern would be in those very countries.[58]

As a result of extensive negotiations two international institutions emerged in 1987 to monitor deforestion. The International Tropical Timber Organization (ITTO) in essence was a commodities organization. Although it promoted the maintenance of the ecological balance among tropical forest states, it also administered the world commodity agreement for tropical timber. The *Tropical Forestry Action Plan* was established to coordinate aid flows in the tropical forest sector with the slow down of deforestation. Unfortunately, neither institution was able to solve the deforestation problem. Since tropical forests lay within the domain of individual states, sovereignty guaranteed states the right to exploit their natural resources as they deemed fit. Additionally, satisfactory resolution of deforestation issues was compounded by international involvement that demanded policies that inhibited economic growth while producing profound social changes.

In sum, international environmental treaty making gained momentum in the later half of the 1980s. While many older international environmental conventions received ratification during the late 1970s and 1980s, five environmental conventions of global significance were negotiated between 1985–1990. The style of international environmental treaties changed in the 1980s. Basic framework treaties supplemented by a program of continuing work to create concrete obligations became the norm of international environmental treaty making during this time. General international environmental principles, such as the polluter pays and precautionary principles, were also incorporated into a broader range of international treaties overall. Finally, in the midst of many successful negotiations there were also some failures: NIEO, UNCLOS, and *Conference on Desertification.*

A Summary of International Environmental Activities in the 1980s

Renewed international and public interest in the environment gave way to increased activity in the international environmental realm through out the 1980s. The UN and UNEP assumed leadership roles in most of the international environmental activities that took place during this decade. Significant progress was made in various international environmental negotiations, including nuclear accidents, hazardous waste, ozone depletion, deforestation, and the conservation of Antarctica. The *World Conservation Strategy,* launched in 1980 by UNEP, IUCN and WWF provided the first detailed stocktaking of the earth's natural resources.

However, not all international environmental activity ended in success. In their assessment of the state of implementation of the Stockholm principles in 1982, the UN determined that little headway had been made in the actual implementation of the recommendations. The *World Charter for Nature,* adopted by UNGA in 1982, appeared to have no visible impact on the behavior of states in the international environmental realm. Although developing countries appeared more willing to participate in environmentally related activities of direct benefit to them, they still lacked the capacity to bring about changes of individual national policies to contribute to wider agreements. Despite the lack of popular concern and capacity to bring about needed change, the heads of the non-aligned movement, whose members were mostly developing countries, met in 1989 Belgrade and devoted three pages of their mission statement to the environment.

As had been the case in the 1960s, the 1980s witnessed growing concern in both the public and international spheres about the long-term impact of human activity on the planet's biosphere. But unlike the 1960s, the end of the decade was accompanied by the feeling across the globe that specific international negotiations to tackle specific environmental issues were no longer enough to stem the tide of environmental degradation.

THE 1990S AND THE INTERNATIONAL ENVIRONMENT

With the advent of the 1990s, the environment became a significant component of international interdependence and interpenetration. As a result of growing interdependence, traditional security concerns were expanded to include environmental concerns. Numerous debates surrounding the environment resurfaced in the international community. Harkening back to the Club of Rome, Northern NGOs and United States green movements called for dramatic changes in the way resources were consumed and effluents were produced if human prospects were not to be seriously endangered by global environmental degradation. Countering this view was that of the "Global Commons" espoused by Garret Hardin. Drawing on the work of Machiavelli, Hardin contended that states would choose to follow their own interests and set aside any concern for global goods. The insights of John Maddox reemerged as many academicians argued that the international community was engaged in a "pantomimic wave of overreaction to some of the supposed dangers of environmental contamination."[59]

The role of the state in the international system also came under scrutiny by those advocating global governance. According to this view, the emergence of a new international agenda was the symptom of the diminishing autonomy of the state. The state was less able to control activities that extended across its borders such as population movement or transboundary pollution. Critics of global governance argued that while there appeared to be an increasing role in the international system for NGOs and other transnational actors, their part had been to act as lobbyists for particular states or as state's agents. While governments often adjusted their policies to accommodate the domestic political pressures of businesses and NGOs, states remained the key players in the international system.

The Road to Rio de Janeiro

As mentioned previously, in 1988, the UNGA called for another environmental summit. The *United Nations Conference on the Environment and Development (UNCED)* was to be held in Rio de Janeiro, Brazil in June 1992. Detailed preparations for the conference began in 1989. The goal of the preparatory process was to have all major documents for the conference ready and agreed to before the conference actually started. Only the major points would be left for participants to settle. The size of the conference agenda was extremely large and complex as it encompassed a full range of environmental and developmental issues. The North sought positive results for their international environmental concerns, while the South looked for outcomes helpful to their developmental ambitions.

The UNCED preparatory committee held four meetings: one in Nairobi (1990); two in Geneva (1991); and, one in New York (1992). These meetings were attended by virtually all UN member states, as well as by a large number of international organizations and NGOs. As it had in the conferences before it, the North-South divide emerged in the preparatory process, and later in the conference itself. The North wanted a set of principles that underlined the need for states to modify their economic and developmental policies to take into account environmental constraints, such as "polluter pays," precautionary principles, as well as population control and natural resource conservation. The South wanted the right to pursue economic development according to their own models. The developing countries also wanted assistance from the North in achieving this end. Since the North was largely responsible for environmental problems, according to their view, then it was their responsibility to take the lead in tackling them. The right of the South to exploit its sovereign natural resources and pursue economic growth through whatever means it thought best was open for adjustment for global environmental ends only to the extent that the North was willing to pay for that adjustment.

There were also differences within camps as well. Foreign aid commitments varied between the developed countries. The United States, the United Kingdom, Germany and Japan only committed low levels of aid, while France, the Netherlands and the Scandinavians were willing to commit higher levels of aid. The United States, the United Kingdom, Germany and Japan saw the needs of the Eastern Europe and the world economic recession as constraining their ability to increase aid levels. France, the Netherlands, and Scandinavia saw this as an opportunity for other western states to increase their aid levels to bring them closer to what these three states were already paying. Developing countries, on the way to industrialization (China, India and Malaysia), tended to place more emphasis on avoidance of unacceptable environmental constraints on their future developmental policies. Poorer and more ecologically exposed countries were more concerned to see western aid increase no matter what the conditions of that assistance entailed.

Maurice Strong was once again appointed as the General Secretary of the summit and proposed two main documents be written for the conference: the *Earth Charter and Agenda 21*. The *Earth Charter* (come to be known as the Rio Declaration of Principles for Action) contained over one hundred and fifty draft principles for future global environmental and developmental action. In addition to reflecting the environmental concerns of the North, the principles encompassed the developmental concerns of South, in addition to a full spectrum of political issues: population growth, the role of women in development, the rights of indigenous peoples, poverty, war, and oppression. The final meeting of the preparatory committee reduced the list to twenty-seven concise and mutually consistent, if vague principles.[60]

Agenda 21 was meant to be an international environmental and developmental action plan for the 21st century. Instead, it became a repository for a full range of national and international environmental and development concerns that individual states wished to see reflected in the outcome of the conference. The North emphasized the shared responsibility of the international community for environmental action, while avoiding any language that might imply an obligation to provide financial relief. The South stressed that environmental damage was the result of over-consumption in the North and poverty in the South. Despite the hopes of many states in the South, *Agenda 21* produced only limited increases in international financial assistance. Because of the diversity of approaches present during the preparatory process, *Agenda 21* did not become the mandatory global action plan that many in the international community had hoped, rather it became a menu from which states could pick and choose appropriate actions given their own priorities.

As mentioned previously, the UN and UNEP wanted to conclude negotiations on the following seven items prior to the Earth Summit: climate change, biodiversity, forests, desertification, institutions, technology, and finance. However, issues of sovereignty and differences of objectives between the North and South made the negotiation process contentious. Although agreements were reached in the areas of climate change and biodiversity, the negotiation of five items could not be resolved before the Earth Summit itself: deserts, forests, institutions, technology, and finance.

The split over target emissions by western states and North-South differences about the amount and management of aid that would be available to assist developing country action in this area hampered the negotiation of the *Framework Convention on Climate Change*. The Intergovernmental Panel on Climate Change was created to establish the scientific consensus necessary for serious negotiations. As Brenton points out, "Given these difficulties, the climate convention was probably only achieved because of the need to have an agreement for Rio."[61]

Although of lower profile, the negotiations surrounding the biodiversity convention were just as fractious. The South was looking for a more substantial return from Northern exploitation of Southern biodiversity. The North was unwilling to make concessions. In the end, the South only took on limited commitments to the treaty.

The issues of deforestation and desertification were politically linked. The North believed negotiations should be launched so as to have a text ready for the *Earth Summit*. Certain forested countries in the South were not so anxious. For the developing countries, any such proposal would not only threaten their sovereignty over the use of their forest resources, it would allow international surveillance of their resource management practices. An impasse between the United States and Malaysia led to the approval of the *Declaration of Principles on Forests* by UNCED, allowing the conference it-self to decide whether that declaration would then initiate negotiation of a convention. Negotiations on desertification resulted in recommendations for action but no strong commitment to the international funding of such undertakings.

In the last meeting of the UNCED preparatory committee the issue of institutions was finally addressed. The North was dissatisfied with existing UN institutional arrangements. Although UNEP had demonstrated the ca-pacity to pilot global environmental business to successful conclusions, it re-mained small, highly technical, and more peripheral to the main political business of the UN than the prominence of the environment justified. Yet, there was little desire in the North for the creation of another expensive agency. On the one hand, the North believed that UNEP should be strength-ened to improve coordination among agencies. Yet, the North feared that such steps would not make the type of political impact the North was seek-ing. Therefore, the North was advocating that UNCED engage in the busi-ness of institution building despite the fact there was the absence of agreement on concrete action in other areas of the environment. States on the way to industrialization, such as China, India and Brazil, did not want the creation of a new international environmental institution because they did not want to succumb to any form of national reporting that such an in-stitution might require. Therefore, the problem of whether to create a new international environmental institution was left for UNCED to resolve.

UNCED was the first major multilateral opportunity for developing countries to renew demands for a significant increase in assistance from de-veloped countries, since the failure of the NIEO in 1980s. According to the South, the North should assist developing countries address environmental degradation that resulted from poverty and underdevelopment because the cooperation of the South was needed to tackle other global environmental problems. Therefore, the South pressed the North on two issues: freer access to western technology and new and additional financial assistance. However, the North's response was reserved. The United States took a hard line stance with the South's demands for aid and technology. According to the US, because technology was in private and not governmental hands, freer access would undermine the incentive for Northern companies to maintain technological innovation if governments were to expropriate their patent rights in the way developing countries seemed to be demanding.[62]

On the issue of finance, Southern ambitions on funding along with increased western public concern regarding environmental issues meant that the North needed to make new money available in order to ensure the Earth Summit's success while avoiding domestic political criticism. The UN's long-standing target (developed countries should give 0.7% of their GNP in foreign aid)[63] was, with the exception of the United States, generally accepted by most of the developed countries. However, no date was provided as to when states would be expected to comply. Since only the Netherlands, Denmark, Sweden, and France had achieved this target, they saw UNCED as an opportunity to increase the contributions of other states. There was no support within the OECD for any new environmental fund and the money being demanded by the South was dismissed as unrealistic. The discussion of finance, then, "amounted to a dialogue of the deaf."[64] The issue went to the *Earth Summit* to be decided.

In 1990, despite disagreement among members of the international community, the Global Environmental Facility (GEF) came into existence as the main financial instrument for global environmental problems in the developing countries. The GEF was to be jointly administered by the World Bank, UNEP, and UNDP. The principle task of the GEF was confined to specific environmental problems such as ozone depletion, climate change, biodiversity, and international water pollution. It would finance only that portion of the costs of environmental projects associated with global rather than local benefits. The developed countries not only saw the GEF as way to draw the developing countries into helping resolve international environmental problems, it was a way to avoid the inefficient and expensive proliferation of single-issue environmental funds along the lines of those established under the Montreal Protocol.

The GEF was not well received in the developing countries. They wanted extra funding for their own developmental projects so that global spending was not high on their list of priorities. They were also nervous about western commitments for funding global environmental programs. First, Eastern Europe and the former Soviet Union, recently liberated from the throws of communism, appeared as potential competitors for western financial assistance. Secondly, the developing countries were afraid that western popular environmentalism would turn into environmental conditionality, which would require money be spent in line with the priorities of the North rather than the developmental priorities of South. Third, the South found the World Bank's role in administering the GEF problematic because they thought the lending criteria would be too tight and insensitive to local economic difficulties. Furthermore, if the GEF was to be the

main financial instrument of climate change and biodiversity, then all signatories of those conventions should have an equal say in the management
fund and just not donors. Hence, the organization of GEF became a key
battleground.

The United Nations Conference on Environment and Development, 1992

At the *United Nations Conference on Environment and Development
(UNCED)* held in Rio de Janiero, Brazil from June 3–14 1992, the international community officially recognized the transboundary or interdependent
nature of environmental degradation and the subsequent implications for international security. Environmental decline was no longer considered a
problem simply for local governments, but one of international concern.
The importance of ecosystems became apparent. The human population
was changing the basic physiology of the planet. Over-exploitation of natural resources was exacting a toll on the availability of finite resources. If left
unchecked, environmental damage would be irreversible.

The Rio conference was the largest gathering of world leaders to ever
take place. Representatives from over one hundred and seventy-eight countries
attended. In addition to state representation, over fourteen hundred NGOs,
one-third of which were from developing countries, sent observers. In all, the
conference had over 35,000 accredited participants and 8,000 journalists.

The conference was accompanied by a variety of events. Four hundred
companies displayed their latest environmental technologies at an industrial
fair known as *EcoTech.*

Various indigenous groups set up a village. Over 18,000 individuals
participated in the *Global Forum,* sponsored by developmental NGOs, scientists, women, and other groups.

NGOs were in close contact with or actually members of national delegations. NGO participation in the preparatory process and conference was
notable because there was a higher proportion of NGOs from the South
than had been present at Stockholm. Interestingly, the gap between the positions argued by Northern environmental NGOs and Southern developmental NGOs was almost as wide as that between their respective
governments.

The agendas of the North and South once again reflected their divergent positions regarding the environment and development. The representatives from the developed countries dwelt on the seriousness of global
environmental problems and need for North-South cooperation. The developing countries focused on domestic environmental problems, especially
those resulting from poverty and underdevelopment, and pressed for more

aid from North. The United States was perceived as a villain because the U.S. refused to accept greenhouse gas targets. It also refused to sign the biodiversity treaty. The United States took a hard line on the availability of new funds. Finally, it was only at the last minute President George H.W. Bush decided to attend the conference.

In regard to international environmental treaties, the biodiversity and climate conventions were opened for signature and each treaty received signatures from nearly 90% of all the countries in attendance.[65] Efforts to produce a declaration on greenhouse gases failed. The *Rio Declaration* was adopted unchanged due to the fact that it was perceived as a delicately balanced text that could provoke a major row between states if it was tampered with. Nearly completed at the final preparatory meeting, the remainder of *Agenda 21* was finalized.

In regard to the five major issues left unresolved at the preparatory process, UNCED took the following steps. In regard to institutions, UNCED approved the creation of the United Nations Commission on Sustainable Development. UNCED also agreed unanimously that there should be a negotiation leading to a desertification convention. They also decided that a convention for deforestation be called. While the wording of many recommendations and documents promoted the transference of more technology, it was clear that intellectual property rights must be maintained. While some western countries made new aid announcements, the question remained whether there would be any real commitment on the long-term expansion of aid levels.

The Lessons of Rio

The products of UNCED are generally seen as disappointing. According to the General Secretary of UNCED, Maurice Strong, there was much "agreement without sufficient commitment."[66] NGOs were critical of the international community's failure to reach a conclusion on forests. The developing countries were unhappy with their failure to achieve concrete long-term commitments on aid. The perceived need to achieve any outcomes and the presence of North-South tensions led to vague language and non-operational texts that would have little direct impact on national policies.

More generally, the first lesson of the *Earth Summit* was the limited ability of global summits to shift significant groups of states from entrenched positions. Perceived national interests seemed to motivate state behavior in the international environmental realm. The second lesson to be learned from UNCED was that without the Rio deadline, the conventions on biodiversity and climate change would not have been completed. Setting deadlines increased the awareness in numerous countries about the seriousness of environmental issues and the importance of adopting policies to resolve them. Third, the international environment found a permanent place on the agendas of major international organizations, such as the UN and its subsidiary agencies (UNDP, World Bank). Finally, the international system has a very short memory. UNCHE and UNCED were only twenty years apart. They covered similar subject matter. They were organized under the same international auspices and with the same Secretary General. One might have thought that UNCED would have picked up where Stockholm left off. However, the negotiators at Rio ignored the lessons of Stockholm,[67] only to rediscover the roadblocks that made Stockholm such hard work.[68] According to Brenton, progress would have been better if the participants at Rio had known more of the history of Stockholm.[69]

The International Environment Post-Rio

Three important international environmental treaties developed out of the UNCED: 1) *Convention on Biological Diversity (CBD)*; 2) *United Nations Framework Convention on Climate Change (UNFCCC)*; and, 3) *United Nations Convention to Combat Desertification (UNCCD)*. The main objective of UNFCCC is "to stabilize greenhouse gas emissions at levels that will prevent dangerous anthropogenic interference with global climate change."[70] One-hundred and eighty-six states had become parties to this convention by December 2001. While the UNFCCC provided the framework for a regulatory structure for greenhouse gases, it was not until 1997 and the negotiation of the *Kyoto Protocol* that actual targets for emissions reductions were spelled out. Although eighty-four states signed the treaty, only 46 had ratified or acceded to the treaty in 2001. The most notable exception was the United States.[71]

The *Convention on Biological Diversity* came into force in 1993. The primary objectives of this treaty are: 1) "the conservation of biological diversity; 2) the sustainable use of its components; and, 3) the fair and equitable sharing of the benefits from the use of genetic resources."[72] One-hundred and eighty-two states had ratified the treaty by December 2001. A supplementary protocol to the treaty emerged in January 2000 in Cartagena, Spain. The *Cartagena Protocol on Biosafety* addressed the "risks posed by cross-border trade and accidental releases of living genetically modified organisms."[73] One-hundred and three states originally signed this protocol, but only nine went on to ratify this agreement as of December 2001.

The purpose of the *United Nations Convention to Combat Desertification* is to support activities related to the control and alleviation of desertification world-wide. The lesser known of the three treaties, this convention became effective in 1996. As of December 2001, 177 states had become parties to the treaty.[74] Despite the large number of parties, this convention has suffered from a lack of support among industrialized nations of the world. The North did not perceive desertification as a global problem and therefore was "unwilling to undertake any financial responsibility for arresting the process of desertification.[75]"

Despite what many deem as post-Rio successes, other attempts by international organizations and NGOs to move the international community forward in the environmental realm were met with lackluster support or inaction. For example, in 1996, the World Bank and World Health Organization issued a joint statement calling for the phase-out of leaded gasoline. According to these institutions, "the health costs of leaded gasoline are far higher than the benefits to a few refiners and gasoline distributors."[76] Only thirty-six countries had totally phased out the use of leaded gasoline by 1999. This number is expected to increase to fifty-five by the year 2005.[77] Unfortunately, this projected estimate still only accounts for only 24% all countries eligible to join the "Unleaded Club."

The election of Bill Clinton to the presidency of the United States reinvigorated hope among environmentalists that the United States would reverse its anti-environmental course and again assume its leadership role in the international environmental realm as it had in the 1970s. On the domestic front, President Clinton wasted no time in promoting the environment. Clinton established the *National Biological Survey* within the United States Department of Interior in 1993. He also signed an executive order restricting logging in old growth forests throughout the United States. A moratorium on the incineration of toxic waste was also invoked in the early years of the Clinton administration. Despite the achievements in the domestic realm, the United States' international environmental record left something to be desired.

American industry had gained momentum in its anti-environmentalist stand. Opposed to the international ban on the shipment of hazardous waste from the developed to developing world, industrial groups within the United States were able to stall the ratification of the *Basel Convention* domestically, while preventing its full implementation internationally in March 1994.[78] Despite the "Climate Change Warning" released by the United Nations Intergovernmental Panel on Climate Change in 1994, American industry once again opposed U.S. support of international climate change initiatives, predicting "disastrous" consequences for the U.S. economy if reductions of CO_2 were enforced.[79]

Not only were policymakers at odds over the role of the United States in the international environmental realm, there also appeared to be a widening gap between environmental groups within the United States. In 1994, the *North American Free Trade Agreement (NAFTA)* highlighted this gap. Groups such as the Environmental Defense Fund and the National Wildlife Federation lent their support to NAFTA because they believed the economic benefits Mexico would derive from this exchange would encourage environmental protection. The Sierra Club and Friends of the Earth opposed NAFTA because of the lack of environmental safeguards.[80] And if this existing "environmental" gap was not enough, in 1995, for the first time in decades, the U.S. Congress came under the control of the Republican Party. Proposed environmental activity in both the domestic and international environmental realms came under attack from member of the Republican Party.[81]

Rio +5

The *Rio +5 Summit* was held in New York City, June 23–27, 1997, five years after UNCED. The goal of the summit was to explore the problems associated with the implementation of *Agenda 21*. The summit concluded that some progress had been made in the area of sustainable development, but for the most part, the targets of *Agenda 21* were a long way from being realized.[82] For instance, during the five years between summits, the international community had experienced increased globalization, specifically in the areas of trade, foreign direct investment and capital markets. While globalization offered many new opportunities, it also presented many challenges especially for the developing world. Therefore, the summit recommended that "national and international environmental and social policies be implemented and strengthened in order to ensure that globalization trends have a positive impact on sustainable development, especially in developing countries."[83]

The summit was also concerned with the growing disparity between the developed and developing world. New economic growth associated with increased globalization was uneven at best and was creating a more significant gap between the least developed states and others. Many states around the world were experiencing worsening economic conditions, an increase in the number of individuals living in poverty, and growing unemployment. These circumstances would lead to additional environmental stresses.

The Summit concluded:

Five years after the United Nations Conference on Environment and Development, the state of the global environment has continued to deteriorate . . . and significant environmental problems remain deeply embedded in the socio-economic fabric of countries in all regions. Some progress has been made. . . .

Overall, however, trends are worsening.84

But growing concern did not necessarily translate into immediate action. The end of the 20th century saw the continuing deterioration of the global environment:

> *Worldwatch* reported that 7 out of 10 scientists believed that the globe was experiencing the largest mass extinction of species in history . . . the population of the earth exceed six million people. Half are living in cities. Almost half (2.8 billion) live on less than $2 a day. UN agencies note that while globalization of trade has helped in some countries, the poor are becoming poorer in both absolute and relative terms.85

2000 AND BEYOND

At the dawn of the new millennium, the United Nations Development Programme stated that:

> one-fifth of the world's inhabitants living in the highest income countries had 86% of the world's Gross Domestic product, 82% pf the world export markets, 68% for foreign direct investment, and 74% pf telephone lines. The bottom one-fifth, in the poorest countries, has about 1% in each category. In the 1990s, more than 80% of foreign direct investment in developing countries and those of Central and Eastern Europe went to just 20 countries, notably China.86

While globalization provides opportunities to enhance people's lives, as the aforementioned statistics suggest the benefits and opportunities of globalization have been unequally distributed. According to UNDP, this unequal distribution of benefits and opportunities is a result of "allowing markets to dominate the process."87 Not only has globalization affected the lives of individuals around the world, it has created new challenges in the environmental realm: "The irony of globalization . . . is that consumption by people in industrialized countries continues to grow, and poverty in the developing regions continues to worsen."88

In an effort to evaluate deteriorating global environmental conditions, a meeting was called of environmental ministers from around the world. The *Global Ministerial Environment Forum* was held May 29–31, 2000. The objectives of this meeting were to: 1) discuss the major international environmental challenges of the new millennium; and, 2) explore strategic policy responses for these challenges.[89] While an important milestone in the international environmental realm, little more than mere proclamations were produced.

The *Global Ministerial Environment Forum* was followed by the *United Nations Millennium Summit* in September 2000. The purpose of the Summit was to find ways to strengthen the role of the United Nations in meeting the challenges of the 21st century. As part of this agenda, issues regarding development and the environment were specifically raised by United Nations Secretary-General Kofi Annan. While members of the United Nations recognized the increasing importance of environmental issues, actual international progress in the environmental realm was less than encouraging. As Annan stated:

> the international community was failing to provide future generations the freedom to sustain their lives on this planet. On the contrary, we have been plundering our children's future heritage to pay for environmentally unsustainable practices in the present.[90]

By the end of President Bill Clinton's term in office, his administration had successfully put into place legislation protecting 58 million acres of national forest from development while creating 8 million acres of land as new national monuments[91]—quite an achievement given the anti-environmental stance of Congress and industry in the United States. The environmental benefits achieved through the Clinton administration's conservation record would soon be over-shadowed by the lack of environmental concern evidenced in the new administration of George W. Bush.

Despite growing international concerns about global warming, the Bush administration adopted an energy plan focused on oil exploration and the new construction of coal and nuclear power plants in May 2001. While Bush mentioned conservation in passing, he also requested funding cuts in the area of the continued environmental research. [92]

2001: Growing Concerns Regarding Global Warming

Concerns regarding global warming continued to escalate through out 2001. In early 2001, *Science* magazine published the results of a satellite survey performed by NASA which showed that over 2,000 of the world's glaciers were shrinking.[93] The International Panel on Climate Change (IPCC) also announced that "evidence regarding climate change was getting stronger, that warming was happening faster, and that consequences looked more severe than first predicted."[94] The expert panel predicted that "average temperatures would rise between 1.4 and 5.8 degrees centigrade over the 21st century."[95]

On June 14, leaders across Europe chastised George W. Bush for the United States' refusal to ratify the *Kyoto Protocol*. In December, the United States National Research Council stated that climate change may arrive more quickly than previously thought, "wreaking sudden and catastrophic damage on people, property, and natural ecosystems."[96] The World Meteorological Organization (WMO) projected that 2001 would be the second warmest year on record. The WMO also reported that nine of the ten warmest years on record had occurred since 1990. This included both 1999 and 2000.

But in the midst of these growing concerns, any chance of environmental reconciliation by the Bush administration was dashed when the United States focused its entire attention on the "war on terrorism," a result of the terrorist attacks against the United States on September 11, 2001. In fact by 2003, the Bush administration had "compiled the most anti-environmental record of any US president in history. Under fire by Bush and Congressional Republicans were the Clean Air Act, the Clean Water Act, the toxic waste Superfund, the Right to Know Act, the Marine Mammal Protection Act and many more." [97]

2002: A Year of Continued Environmental Decline

The year began with a stunning report that analyses of satellite images revealed Mexico had lost almost 3 million acres of forest and jungle each year in the seven year period of 1993–2000.[98] This was nearly twice the amount of deforestation officials had previously estimated. Also in January, Greenpeace issued a statement claiming that the Japanese government was prepared to restart whaling by any means necessary: "it's buying votes and ultimately it's buying the world's whales."[99] The group urged that a closer investigation of "vote buying" in the International Whaling Commission be undertaken in an effort to prevent Japan from overturning the moratorium on commercial whaling in place since 1986.[100]

The *World Summit on Sustainable Development* (AKA Rio +10) was held in Johannesburg, South Africa August 26—September 4, 2002. The goal of the summit was to address the disappointing results in the implementation of sustainable development internationally. It was hoped that once and for all an environmental summit of this importance would produce actions and results rather than merely political debate. But according to Greenpeace International, "governments, led by the United States, Australia and Canada, are 'working overtime' to ensure that the summit does not adopt any real commitments on essential matters like water, energy, health, agriculture and biodiversity."[101]

International organizations were not alone in their dissatisfaction—many states were unhappy with the outcome of Rio +10. President Hugo Chavez of Venezuela stated that WSSD "had turned out to be a 10-day 'dialogue of the deaf.'"[102] The *Friends of the Earth International,* advocated the halt to environmental summits, stating that "world leaders have sold out to the World Trade Organization and big business. They have done nothing for the poor."[103]

The summit did set a number of goals: 1) cut in half by 2015 the 2.4 billion people without sanitation in the Third World; 2) minimize harmful effects from chemicals production by 2020; and, 3) halt the decline in fish stocks by 2015.[104] But in order to reach these goals, increased aid from the developed world would be required. This was not something much of the developed world wished to contribute to. Once again, the North-South divide reared its ugly head at WSSD.

LESSONS OF HISTORY

The three biggest international environmental events to date are the *United Nations Conference on the Human Environment (1972), the United Nations Conference on Environment and Development (1992), and the World Summit on Sustainable Development (2002).* Each conference provided a snapshot of the state of global environmental attitudes at the time they took place and together offered a rather clear view of what changed, and what did not change in the 30 years between them.

International Cohesion in the Environmental Realm

Environmental issues have continued to impinge upon the international system for the past thirty years. Although states may not always agree as to the appropriate remedies for environmental degradation, there has been greater international cohesion in the environmental realm overall. The role of the United Nations system and the maturation of the negotiation process, itself, have assisted states in "coming together" to address international environmental concerns.

The original mandate of UNEP was that of coordinator and catalyst for international environmental action within the UN. Since its inception at Stockholm, UNEP has grown from a marginal player to "principal midwife"[105] of international action on environmental problems. Even though UNEP has yet to become "the chief coordinator" of international environmental activity, it has become a catalyst for international environmental progress.

The globalization of news and the open, public style of the negotiation process are the key innovations of Stockholm. In recent years, the procedure of negotiation has become "process oriented," whereby states: 1) construct small secretariats to administer agreements and organize meetings; and, 2) meet regularly to strengthen their commitments. On the one hand, the single-issue focus of more recent environmental agreements has been criticized as inefficient and inadequate to enforce compliance. On other hand, they have performed well because they: 1) deal with heterogeneous topics; 2) are free from political crosscurrents and over bureaucratization; 3) are helped by NGOs who have gained greater influence over the decision-making process and who monitor agreements; and, 4) allow the mobilization of public opinion in countries with environmentally advanced agendas.

The Expanding Role of Non-Governmental Organizations

The role of NGOs has expanded over the past thirty years. NGOs continue to shape public opinion and influence governments. They help marshal international cohesion on environmental matters by assisting with the negotiation process and setting international environmental agendas. Furthermore, NGOs help the international community monitor environmental agreements. NGOs also distribute more funds in developing countries than the World Bank.[106] Although their influence reached new heights during the negotiation process of UNCED, this does not mean NGO influence is critical. Although their influence may diminish as public attention diminishes, this does not mean their contributions are not substantial.

The South and the Environment

Southern behavior toward environmental issues has changed relatively little from UNCHE in 1972. Environmental decision-making is a top-down process whereby governments initiate both domestic and international environmental action. Governments in the South have traditionally assigned higher priority to economic development while the environment remains of secondary importance. It is unlikely that developing governments will abandon their efforts to achieve higher levels of development for environmental reasons any time soon. If the developing countries follow the western trajectory, it seems reasonable to conclude that as these countries prosper, they will devote more attention to environmental problems.

The growth of scientific knowledge and increasing international awareness has helped the developing world identify environmental problems which are in their own interests to confront, and as a result, have begun to do so. They have also benefited from analyzing the Northern experience, and are likely to experience less pollution with increasing levels of industrialization. The real problem in the developing world is those countries not experiencing growth, such as South Asia and sub-Sahara Africa. These countries are dragged down by environmental degradation they cannot solve. Rapid population growth, over-intensive agriculture, and soil degradation exacerbate already dire environmental conditions. The poorer countries attract little attention from the North because they are experiencing "local" rather than "global" environmental problems.

The Environment, Democracy and Free Markets

It has also been suggested that countries with prosperous economies and democratic systems of government are better equipped to face the environmental problems confronting them:

> Twenty years have shown that there are clear implications in the relationship between environmental protection and political freedom. The impulse for environmental protection has been very much a democratic phenomena.[107]

Why is this the case? First, freedom of association, speech, and publication allows public pressure to be channeled toward the government and democracy is responsive to public pressure. [108] Second there seems to be a relationship between prosperity, democracy and environmental action. Once people have achieved a certain level of material affluence, they turn their attention from immediate needs to long-term needs, of which the environment is one.[109] As countries become richer, they acquire the administrative systems to enforce environmental controls and thus protect the common good against individual self-interest. The absence of prosperity in the developing world, on the other hand, has produced resistance to agreements perceived as constraining future prospects for economic growth. Developing countries also have weak administrative infrastructures that inhibit their ability to enforce the environmental laws they have instituted. Furthermore, democracies have developed a substantial body of environmental action and collaboration. They have historically tackled domestic pollution and shown greater determination to prevent environmental degradation.

Finally, although environmentalists assert that free trade is damaging to the environment because it encourages the exploitation of developing countries resources and the spread of industry to laxer environmental regimes,[110] economists argue free market mechanisms provide less environmentally damaging practices than other forms of economic activity. Price signals, for example, have produced less wasteful and environmentally destructive allocation of resources. Channels for public and consumer pressure are available to offset producer pressures which otherwise tend to dominate governmental decision making and which tend to be deployed in opposition to environmental regulation.[111] Prosperity, another characteristic of free markets, allows states, especially those in the South, to develop the capacity to advance their environmental concerns in the international system while resolving environmental problems in the domestic context. Free markets, then, raise global environmental standards because "goods are produced where it is most efficient to do so, rather than where subsidies and duties push them. Thus under free trade a given level of world product will consume less resources and produce less pollution than when trade is distorted."[112] Since economic growth is likely to continue into the next century, the question becomes whether free trade will be more or less environmentally friendly.[113]

Global Governance or the Primacy of the State?

As mentioned previously in this text, the role of the state in the international system has come under increasing scrutiny by global governance scholars. According to this view, the emergence of a new international agenda that includes the environment is the result of the diminishing capacity of the state to control transboundary activities. In other words, the erosion of sovereignty is occurring as a result of increased interdependence in the international system.

Despite growing interdependence in the international system, the state remains the primary actor and locus of political loyalties in the international system. So long as international environmental accords are negotiated by states, national interest will continue to play a large part in deciding the outcome. States will pursue their own individual national interests and thus find it difficult to cooperate for the common good. This trend is likely to continue as the number of states in the international system grows. With the increase of active participants in the international system, the number of obstacles and costs associated with resolving international environmental problems will also increase. The capacity of the international system to monitor and enforce obligations on states will be reduced, not to mention the mechanical problems of negotiating conventions with a large number of states. Therefore, "common interests" are likely to become remote from the interests of individual states. The bottom line is that so long as states are the center of the decision-making process in the international system, "perceived national interests rather than the *Stockholm Declaration of Principles* or the intervention of UNEP has been the prime mover of international environmental cooperation."[114]

CONCLUSION

Even though significant progress has been made in the international environmental arena in the years since Stockholm, there is still much to achieve. By examining the historical and analytical context of international environmentalism, it becomes clear that state behavior in the international environmental realm is influenced by a variety of factors including: structural characteristics of the international system; economic considerations; equity issues; environmental treaty type; and, governmental type. In order to determine their usefulness and accuracy in explaining state behavior, it is now time to subject these variables to empirical analyses.

Chapter Four

Determinants of State Behavior in the International Environment: Becoming a Party to International Environmental Treaties

A mythic "humanity" is created—irrespective of whether we are talking about oppressed ethnic minorities, women, Third World people, or people of the First World—in which everyone is brought into complicity with powerful corporate elites in producing environmental dislocations. A new kind of biological "original sin" is created in which a vague group of animals called "Humanity" is turned into a destructive force that threatens the survival of the living world.

—Murray Bookchin, (1990) *Remaking Society: Pathways to a Green Future*, p. 9–10.

The purpose of this chapter is to provide an overview of the data-making procedures and methodology used to evaluate the ability of international relations theory to account for the probability that states will become parties to international environmental treaties. This chapter is divided into five sections. Section one offers a justification for this study. The second section identifies the spatial-temporal domain of this undertaking. Section three not only identifies the outcome and predictor variables used in this study, it also provides a discussion of the data-making procedures. Section four provides an overview of the methodological approach used to analyze the data. Finally, section five discusses the limitations of this study.

JUSTIFICATION OF THIS STUDY

Despite the growing recognition of the importance of environmental issues for international relations, current research on international environmental politics is insufficient. As mentioned previously in this text, although scholars in the field of international relations believe that there is an appropriate role for international relations theory in analyzing global environmental concerns,[1] the existing literature is predominantly descriptive or prescriptive rather than analytical.[2] The analytical work that has been done " . . . has been limited to the institutionalist vein, with little work presented from the neo-realist camp."[3]

The need for cooperative strategies and solutions to international environmental problems, as reflected in "regime theory," has become a central theme in major scholarly works on international environmental security. For the most part then, the study of international environmental politics has become a process of finding appropriate cooperative or institutional mechanisms to overcome the collective action problem:

> The measure of solutions to international environmental problems thus became the efficiency of the mechanism for dealing with overcoming collective action problems, rather than the viability of the political settlement underlying the mechanism.[4]

While this literature has provided insight into state behavior in the international environmental realm, it fails to acknowledge that international environmental issues are as heavily politicized as most other kinds of international issues. To ignore traditional power politics is highly unrealistic[5] because there has been little evidence provided by the scholarly community that would support the dismissal of neo-realism as an appropriate research program through which to examine international environmental issues. If the task at hand is to determine the usefulness of existing research programs in explaining state behavior in the international environmental realm, the abandonment of traditional research programs without adequate empirical analysis will not expand our knowledge and understanding of the field.

Drawing on the previous chapters of this study, it becomes clear that international relations theory is amenable to the historical experiences of states in the international environmental realm. I therefore have chosen variables from the variants of international relations theory to determine their usefulness and accuracy in explaining state behavior in regard to international environmental treaties. More specifically, this study will analyze whether the following variables influence the probability a state will become a party to an international environmental treaty: 1) international environmental treaty type; 2) military interests of the state; 3) equitable distribution of the costs associated with an international environmental treaty; 4) power distribution in the international system; 5) governmental type of a state; and, 6) vulnerability to an environmental problem.

The importance of exploring this question is twofold. First, international environmental treaties have become the main tool through which states in the international system address environmental concerns.[6] Identification of those factors that enhance the likelihood of a state becoming a party to an international environmental treaty will allow for their inclusion in forthcoming negotiations and thus ensure a better record of agreement in the future.

Secondly, there is no set time limit for states to become parties to international environmental agreements. As will be discussed later in this chapter, a treaty usually remains open for signature for a period of twelve months. However, additional methods, such as ratification, acceptance, approval or accession allow states to become bound by the terms of the treaty after that initial period. The states that comprise the international system are hardly static entities. The attributes of states can change over time. For instance, states may move toward more open political systems. They may increase their level of economic development. A state may even become more vulnerable to an existing environmental problem over time. Consequently, it seems reasonable to conclude that a state's decision to become a party to an international environmental treaty may change with time as a result of changing attributes. Therefore, to capture these changes, the attributes of states must be examined over time to determine if such changes alter the likelihood a state will become a party to an international environmental treaty.

SPATIAL-TEMPORAL DOMAIN OF THIS STUDY

The spatial-temporal domain of this study encompasses international environmental treaties and sovereign states between the years of 1972 through 2000. For the purpose of this study, an international environmental treaty will be defined as a treaty that deals with global environmental issues that either affect the global commons or put the common heritage of mankind at risk.[7] International environmental treaties are open to signature, ratification, acceptance, accession or succession by all sovereign states and members or associate members of the United Nations or its specialized agencies.

In determining which international environmental treaties would be included in this study, the *United Nations Register of International Treaties and Other Agreements in the Field of the Environment* (2000) was first consulted.[8] Using 1972 as the starting point and 2000 as the end point of this study, the United Nations register revealed that there were one hundred and eight international environmental treaties available for possible inclusion in this analysis. These treaties were then examined to determine whether they were international or regional[9] in orientation. Of the 108 environmental treaties available for inclusion, seventy were identified as being regional treaties, while the remaining thirty-eight treaties met the above-mentioned definition of "international." Therefore, the population of environmental treaties examined in this study consists of thirty-eight treaties.[10]

Only sovereign states,[11] with populations of one million or more are included in this study.[12] Sovereignty was established for each state using data from the following sources: Bruce Russet, J. David Singer and Melvin Small (1968) "National Political Units in the Twentieth Century: A Standardized List," APSR, 62 (4), pp. 932–951; and, J. David Singer and Melvin Small (1993) *National Material Capabilities Data Set.* The population for each state was compiled using the following source: the United Nations Population Division (1992) *Interpolated National Populations.* The year in which each state entered into the international system and the year in which the population of each state reached one million were compared to determine the years that each state would be included in this study.[13]

The *United Nations Conference on the Human Environment* in 1972 was not only the first international environmental summit to be held; it also ". . . laid the intellectual foundations for the emergence of a sustained debate over the earth." [14] In fact, of the 170 international environmental treaties adopted, over 2/3 of these treaties were adopted since Stockholm in 1972.[15] Given the importance of the *Stockholm Conference* in bringing environmental concerns to the attention of members of the international community, 1972 was chosen as the starting point for my examination of international environmental treaties. The endpoint of this study is 2000. This endpoint was chosen because there is a general lack of updated information regarding states becoming parties to international environmental treaties after this date.

DATA-MAKING: IDENTIFICATION AND OPERATIONALIZATION OF THE VARIABLES

Outcome Variable

The Probability a State Will Become a Party to an International Environmental Treaty

Before a global environmental treaty becomes binding on the contracting parties, the treaty must be adopted by the conference of delegates representing the states that negotiated the treaty. These countries may then sign the treaty while it is open for signature, which usually encompasses a twelve-month period. While the signature "does not establish the consent of the country to be bound by the treaty, it does qualify the signatory state to proceed to ratification, acceptance, approval, or accession to the treaty."[16]

Ratification "defines the international act whereby a state indicates its consent to be bound to a treaty of the parties intended to show their consent by such an act." [17] Ratification allows states the necessary time to seek approval of the treaty through national procedures and to enact the necessary national legislation to give effect to that treaty.[18] Acceptance and Approval have the same legal effect as ratification, but are used in instances where national procedures do not require a treaty to be ratified by the Head of State.[19] Accession, on the other hand, permits states to accept or become a party to a treaty, which has already been negotiated and signed by other countries.[20] It, too, has the same legal effect as ratification. For the purposes of this study, the term "become a party to" will be used to indicate a country's willingness to be bound to the terms of a treaty regardless of the specific procedure used to signify that willingness.

The probability a state will become a party to an international environmental treaty is the outcome variable of this study. While it might seem reasonable to assume that a signature to a treaty indicates a state's intent to become bound by that treaty, it might very well be the case that a signature to a treaty may be nothing more than a rhetorical commitment. One should not infer that all signatories can or will assume the responsibility for environmentally sound management of their natural resources or mediate conflicts over competing uses of those resources. Becoming a party to a treaty, on the other hand, suggests a state's commitment to the terms of the treaty, as well as its willingness to create the national legislation and institutions necessary to comply with those terms. In other words, "becoming a party to an international environmental treaty" gets to the heart of the issue. By examining "the probability a state will become a party to an international environmental treaty," I will be able to account for a greater range of state behavior in the international environmental realm. State behavior in this regard was compiled from the "Party Information" provided by the *United Nations Register of International Treaties and Other Agreement in the Field of the Environment* (2000) and the Consortium for International Earth Science Information Network (2000) ENTRI Database for the thirty-eight international environmental treaties under consideration in this study.

Predictor Variables

Environmental Treaty Type: Pollution Control versus
Resource Management Treaties

There is a vast array of international environmental issues and international treaties for their resolution. Therefore, it is impractical to put all of the issues into the same category for examination. By doing so, differences in the way individual states may approach the particular issues at hand may be obscured. By unpacking environmental issues, one would be able to determine whether different issues elicit different behavior on the part of states in the international system. There are two categories into which international environmental treaties are often placed: pollution control and resource management.

Resource Management, in this context, refers to the control of abrupt changes in ecosystems or the preservation from loss, damage or neglect through controlled use and systematic protection. In other words, taking the appropriate measures to "increase the efficiency of capital accumulation to maximize production, whether trees or animals."[21]

Pollution is defined as the "introduction by man into the environment of substances or energy liable to cause hazards to human health, harm to living resources and ecological systems, damage to structures or amenity, or interference with legitimate uses of the environment."[22] Therefore, pollution control is defined as the ability to exercise authority to constrain, reduce or eliminate activities that contribute to environmental degradation. It is also important to note that the costs of pollution control treaties are generally more expensive than the costs of resource management treaties because pollution control treaties often entail the added costs associated with clean up or reductions that directly impact a state's economic competitiveness. Despite a state's willingness to recognize the need for pollution control, pollution control may actually be difficult to achieve because of the additional costs of such policies and the constraints these policies place on free market forces.[23]

Given the fact that pollution control treaties are more likely to impose constraints on a state's economic competitiveness, the following hypothesis was tested: *Hypothesis 1- There is an increased probability a state will become a party to an international environmental treaty if that treaty is a resource management treaty.*

Table 4.1 Classification of International Environmental Treaties by Treaty Type, 1972–2000

	Resource Management Treaties	Pollution Control Treaties
1972–1979	6	8
1980s	4	12
1990–2000	4	4

International Environmental Treaty's Impact on State's Military Interests

Within the neo-realist framework, military or security issues are identified as those most salient to sovereign states. The military interest of the state involves enhancing the state's position in the international system with regard to its military (men, conventional and unconventional weapons) and in affairs of war. In other words, a state wants to ensure that its military position is not reduced relative to others in the international system. Therefore, states are unlikely to engage in international activities that threaten to compromise their military position vis-à-vis other states in the international arena.

Would this behavior carry over into the international environmental realm? Mathias Finger noted: "The more important the military-industrial complex is within a country, the more likely it is that state will act as a protector of its military rather than as a protector of the biosphere."[24] Therefore, international environmental treaties' expected impact on states' military interests were tested.

In order to determine whether or not an international environmental treaty requires a state to alter its behavior with regard to its military interests, the texts of the treaties were examined in order to determine what impact, if any, the treaty had on the expected behavior of the state. After examining the texts, it was determined that five of the thirty-eight treaties could possibly impact the military behavior of states.[25]

In addition to international environmental treaties being coded as having an impact on the military behavior of a state, states were also coded as to whether or not they possessed nuclear technology and/or weapons, biological weapons technology, or the military capabilities necessary to engage in modification of the environment.[26]

Table 4.2 International Environmental Treaties Impacting the Military Interests of Nation-States

---

Convention on the Prohibition of the Development, Production and Stockpiling of Bacteriological (Biological) and Toxin Weapons, and on their Destruction (London, 1972)
Convention on the Prohibition of Military or Any Other Hostile Use of the Environmental Modification Techniques (Geneva, 1976)
Convention on the Physical Protection of Nuclear Material (Vienna, 1979)
Convention on Early Notification of a Nuclear Accident (Vienna, 1986)
Convention on Assistance in the Case of a Nuclear Accident or Radiological Emergency (Vienna, 1986).

The following hypothesis was tested: *Hypothesis 2—There is a decreased probability a state will become a party to an international environmental treaty if that treaty requires behavioral changes or imposes constraints on the military interests of the state.*

Equitable Distribution of Treaty Costs

The purpose of this variable is to measure whether or not an international environmental treaty impacts a state's economic interests by examining whether the treaty allows for the equitable distribution of the costs associated with the adoption and implementation of said treaty. International environmental treaties are complex instruments because the solutions offered by such treaties are often constrained by the costs associated by employing new technologies. Furthermore, states are concerned with the fair allocation of these costs in order to prevent free-riding. As Hurrell and Kingsbury note, "Negotiations focus on the allocation of losses incurred through environmental regulations not with the gains resulting from wiser resource management."[27]

Not only do states fear exploitation, they are also concerned that their partners in a cooperative effort might cheat or fail to live up to their agreements—allowing their partners to gain more from cooperation than they do. For this reason, equity issues can impede cooperative undertakings. If a state concerned with equity issues can be guaranteed that the distribution of costs associated with the solutions proposed by an international environmental treaty are evenly dispersed among participants, and other states will behave according to the rules established in a cooperative agreement, there is an increased likelihood that cooperation will ensue. In other words, equitable burden sharing and increased transparency may foster cooperation. Increased transparency can be achieved through the presence of mechanisms, which would allow for the monitoring of another state's behavior in order to prevent cheating, deception and noncompliance. In sum, classic equity issues—whom benefits and who bears the burden of the costs and risks—are likely to decide whether or not a state will become a party to an international environmental treaty.

For the purposes of this study, then, "equitable distribution" has been defined as the equal sharing of treaty costs and benefits among parties to that treaty. In order to determine whether or not the costs associated with international environmental treaties are equitably distributed, the language of the treaty texts for each of the treaties included in this study were examined to identify the primary party/parties responsible for funding the costs associated with treaty adoption and implementation.[28]

Table 4.3 Number of International Environmental Treaties Requiring Equitable Distribution of Costs, Technology Transfers and Monitoring Mechanisms, 1972–2000

Requirement	Number of Treaties
Equitable Distribution of Costs	7
Technology Transfers	14
Monitoring Mechanisms	13

Technological transfers[29] serve as another indicator of the equitable distribution of costs associated with treaty adoption and implementation. Therefore, a variable measuring the presence or absence of technological transfers was created.[30] Finally, a variable to measure the presence or absence of monitoring mechanisms was created in order to determine whether monitoring mechanisms influence state behavior in the international environmental realm. The treaty texts were once again examined to obtain this information.[31]

The following hypotheses were tested in regard to equity and transparency: *Hypothesis 3—There is an increased probability a state will become a party to an intenational environmental treaty if the costs associated with that treaty are equitably distributed among parties to the treaty; Hypothesis 4—There is a decreased probability a nation- state will become a party to an international environmental treaty if that treaty requires the state to transfer technology to another state; and, Hypothesis 5—There is an increased probability a state will become a party to an international environmental treaty if that treaty provides mechanisms for monitoring state* behavior.

Power Distribution in the International System

Power is a key concept in structural explanations of world politics. In an international system characterized by anarchy, self-help, and the security dilemma, power not only determines the position of states within the system, it ensures their survival. Power also defines the relationship between states. In other words, power not only determines how states influence each other, but how they may react to that influence as well. Power, then, will be used as a variable to measure whether or not more powerful states behave differently than less powerful states in the realm of international environmental politics.

For the purposes of this study, power is defined as "the ability of the nation to manipulate its international environment, particularly its ability to influence the behavior of other nations and to withstand unwelcome influence on their part."[32] In other words, power might be though of as "the capacity of the nation to control the behavior of others in accordance with its own ends."[33] Based on the work of Organski and Kugler,[34] power is measured by the following equation:

$$\text{Power} = \text{population} \times \text{GNP/population} = \text{GNP}^{[35]}$$

While this equation does not directly measure the capability of the political system to do its job, it is the preferred measure because: 1) the data available is reliable for that measure; 2) it is parsimonious; and, 3) it is theoretically attractive.[36] For these reasons, then, Gross National Product (GNP) was utilized as a measure of power in this study in order to determine whether or not a states' power position within the international system influences its behavior in the international environmental realm.[37]

The first area of analysis is the role "great powers"[38] play in the international environmental realm. If "great powers" are indeed the most powerful states in the international system, it follows they have the greatest ability to influence other states. When examining the negotiation of international agreements, Guruswamy noted that power was an important variable to consider:

> International agreements can be rendered ineffective by the refusal of powerful countries to adopt them and bring in the necessary national legislation to implement them. Since international law is consensual, it cannot be created without the support of the powerful nations.[39]

"Great powers," then, not only have the ability to influence the actual negotiation of international environmental treaties, they may also exert influence over less powerful states in the accession processes. In order to determine whether or not "great powers" influence a states' decision to become a party to an international environmental treaty one must first examine the historical context in which the treaties were negotiated to see what role the "great powers" had in the negotiation process.[40] The following hypothesis was tested in this study: *Hypothesis 6—There is an increased probability a state will become a party to an international environmental treaty if "a great power" or "great powers" assume a leadership role in the negotiation process.*

The second area of analysis involving the function of power in international environmental politics involves the role of GNP in a states' decision to become a party to an international environmental agreement. As discussed in Chapter Three, in the early 1970s, it became apparent that developed and developing states had varying viewpoints regarding the relationship between the environment and development. According to states of the global South, their environmental problems were related to poverty. There appeared to be too little industry by which to stimulate the necessary economic and social growth to alleviate impoverished conditions. Therefore, some pollution seemed to be worth the price of increasing the overall living standard in these countries. Consequently, the South was unwilling to compromise needed economic growth for more stringent environmental standards. Additionally, given these low levels of economic development, Southern states did not posses the financial resources necessary to take the appropriate actions required to promote environmentally sustainable development. States of the global North, on the other hand, believed that developmental policies in the South should be significantly altered in order to prevent further environmental decline. This debate continues to dominate international discussions of the environment even today.

Accordingly, it seems reasonable to test the influence of GNP on a state's decision to become a party to an international environmental treaty with time. For operational and analytical purposes, the classification scheme developed by the World Bank[41] was adopted for the purpose of categorizing states as low-income economies, middle- income economies, or high-income economies.[42] The classification of economies was established on an annual basis from 1972–2000 using data provided by the World Bank.[43] The following hypothesis was tested: *Hypothesis 7—There is an increased probability that a state will become a party to an international environmental treaty if that state has a high- income economy.*

Governmental Type

As discussed elsewhere, scholarly attention has been focused on the specific internal attribute of governmental type in recent years. The proposed relationship between democratic governmental types and pacific behavior in the international arena is noteworthy.[44] One might infer from this proposed relationship that democratic or "more free" governmental forms may influence state behavior in the realm of the international environment as well. Unfortunately, as Gleditsch and Sverdrup point out:

> there have been few theoretical studies and empirical investigations on the influence of the political system on environmental performance. More emphasis has been placed on the impact of the economic system, on environmental negotiations, diplomacy and formation of international regimes.[45]

Not only are discussions of the influence of governmental type on the environment absent from the literature on democracy and international relations theory, they are absent from international environmental politics literature as well. Despite the lack of comprehensive studies regarding governmental type and international environmental behavior, many authors cite the existence of good environmental records, the existence of a knowledgeable citizenry, of powerful NGOs as proof that more open or free governmental types engage in more environmentally responsible behavior than do less free governmental types. Based on this assertion, it seems reasonable to assume that "more open or free" governmental types are more likely to become parties to international environmental treaties than "less free" governmental types. Additional research into the relationship between governmental type and the environment could further enhance and clarify our understanding of state behavior in the international environmental arena.

In an attempt to explore this relationship, a variable reflecting the governmental type of a state (based upon levels of freedom[46]) was used to measure the influence of governmental type on the probability a state will become a party to an international environmental treaty with time. Data establishing the level of political freedom for each of the states included in this study was collected from Freedom House for the years 1972–2000.[47] The following hypothesis was tested in this study: *Hypothesis 8—The greater freedom a state has, the more likely the state will become a party to an international environmental treaty.*

Vulnerability to Environmental Problem

The work of Volker von Prittwitz suggested that a state's willingness to engage in the creation and implementation of international environmental policy was directly related to whether a state has polluter interests (advantages gained from the continuation of polluting activities) or victim interests (the perceived adverse impact of pollutant activities undertaken in one's own country or abroad).[48] Drawing on the work of von Prittwitz, Sprinz and Vaahtoranta concluded that one of the determinants of a country's willingness to engage in the regulation of international air pollution was a country's "ecological vulnerability," or vulnerability to damage resulting from pollution.[49] This conclusion finds support in the work Repetto and Lash, who concluded that in the case of climate change:

> Although international cooperation is essential, countries' interests differ depending on whether they have coal, oil, gas, etc.; whether industries are energy, labor-, or technology intensive. And whether geography, current climate, and economic structure make them more or less vulnerable to the foreseeable effect of climate change.[50]

Using the concept of ecological vulnerability presented by Prittwitz, Sprinz, and Vaahtorant, the variable "vulnerability" was created in order to determine whether or not a state's vulnerability to damage resulting from pollution or unsustainable resource management influences its decision to become a party to an international environmental treaty. For the purpose of this study, vulnerability is defined as an "actor's liability to suffer costs imposed by external events even after [its] policies have been altered.[51]

"The Overview of Regional Status and Trends"[52] for the years 1972–2000 proved an invaluable source for establishing a state's vulnerability to a particular environmental problem. This document not only identifies various environmental problems facing the international community as a whole, it establishes levels of vulnerability to those problems using a regional classification scheme and environmental data collected by the United Nations Environmental Programme. In order to utilize this information, each state was first coded as to its regional location.[53] Once regional classification was established, states were then coded as to their vulnerability to particular environmental problems on an annual basis.[54] Therefore, each state was coded as to it regional location and particular vulnerability based on that location to a specific environmental problem. It is also important to note that when the international environmental treaties included in this study addressed issues of marine pollution and global climate change, it was necessary to invoke a slightly different coding scheme because coastal states are more vulnerable to the consequences of marine pollution and global climate change than are non-coastal states.[55] Therefore, regardless of regional location, all coastal states were coded as vulnerable in regard to international environmental treaties that addressed marine pollution or climate change. The following hypothesis was tested in regard to ecological vulnerability: *Hypothesis 9—There is an increased probability that a state will become a party to an international environmental treaty if that state is more vulnerable to the particular environmental problem addressed in that treaty.*

METHODOLOGY

As discussed previously in this chapter, the variables chosen for analysis in this study were selected based on a review of existing international relations theory and the historical experiences of states in the international environmental realm. To test hypotheses on when states became parties to international environmental treaties, the data had to be set up to reflect the values of the variables on a yearly basis. Columns were first set up to identify the international environmental treaties included in this study, identify the countries eligible to become parties to the specified international environmental treaties, the years for which the international environmental treaty was open for each state to become a party to it; the year in which the state actually became a party to a particular treaty; and, columns for each of the predictor variables.

Each of the treaties included in this study was assigned a number from one to thirty-eight. States eligible to become parties to a given international environmental treaty were then listed in alphabetical order.[56] "Treaty year" is defined as the year in which an international environmental treaty became open for states to become parties to it, followed by the years it remained open until a state became or did not become a party to the treaty. The temporal domain for this study (1972–2000) is reflected in this column. The next column, "year open," is simply the way in which "treaty year" is coded for the purpose of analysis. Zero (0) represents the year in which the international environmental treaty becomes available for a state to become a party to it. The subsequent numbers (e.g., 1, 2, 3, etc.) reflect the number of years the international environmental treaty remained open for party membership. The "year of party" column is used to identify and analyze the specific year in which a state became a party to a specific international environmental treaty. In this column, zero (0) represents the failure of the state to become a party to an international environmental treaty in that given year. One (1) represents the year in which a state became a party to the treaty under examination. The predictor variables have been coded using the coding rules discussed previously in this chapter.

Once the dataset had been set up according to these guidelines, a binary dependent variable model (logit) was used for the purpose of analyzing the data. In this class of models, the dependent variable is dichotomous. In other words, y may take on only two values: y is either a zero (0) or a one (1).[57] The resulting coefficients from the estimated equation indicate the probability of a given outcome—either zero (0) or one (1). A simple linear regression

Table 4.4 Example of Data Set Up*

Treaty #	Country	Treaty Year	Year Open	Year of Party	Treaty Type	Military Impact	Equitable Distribution	Monitoring Mechanism
1	Afghan	1972	0	0	1	0	1	0
1	Afghan	1973	1	0	1	0	1	0
1	Afghan	1974	2	0	1	0	1	0
1	Afghan	1975	3	1	1	0	1	0

* Not all predictor variables included in this particular study are represented above. This table is only for the purposes of illustration.

of y on x is not appropriate, since among other things, the fitted value of y from a simple linear regression is not restricted to lie between zero and one.

LIMITATIONS OF THIS STUDY

As mentioned previously, this study was a preliminary investigation of the ability of international relations theory to account for state behavior in the international environmental realm. Therefore, this study will provide the groundwork for additional studies. In addition to the limitations imposed on this study by the methodology chosen for the purpose of analysis, several other limitations also deserve mention here.

This study does not examine those negotiations in the international environmental realm that were not conclusive. Appropriate documentation and data regarding non-conclusive negotiations were not available, and therefore, one cannot appropriately analyze state behavior in these instances. The findings of this study can only account for state behavior where negotiations ended with a formal agreement or treaty involving international environmental issues.

International environmental treaties are open to ratification, acceptance, accession and succession by states for an unlimited period of time. Due to the fact that this study encompasses a period of 28 years (1972–2000), this study cannot account for a state's decision to accede to an international environmental treaty beyond this time constraint. Also, only sovereign states with populations of one million or more are included in this study. Therefore, the findings of this study cannot be generalized beyond this population.

The classification of environmental treaties into two types, resource management and pollution control, is subjective in nature, because as with any typology, environmental challenges have multiple dimensions and therefore are subject to classification in more than one type. Not only did I use the definitions of these two types of treaties to guide me in the placement of the treaties into classifications; I have also looked to the major content of each treaty to help place the treaty in the appropriate category. Despite these limitations, the next chapter of this study will chapter provide an empirical analysis of those factors thought to influence the probability a state will become a party to an international environmental treaty with time.

Chapter Five
Becoming a Party to International Environmental Treaties: An Analysis

When you say you agree to a thing in principle you mean you have not
the slightest intention of carrying it out in practice.

—Otto von Bismarck

The purpose of this chapter is to provide an empirical analysis of those factors
thought to influence the probability a state will become a party to an international environmental treaty. This chapter is divided into three sections. The
first section will provide a summary of the parameters of this study. The second section will provide analyses of the estimation results for each of the predictor variables. In section three, I will provide my preliminary conclusions.

PARAMETERS OF THIS STUDY

The spatial-temporal domain of this study covers international environmental treaties and sovereign states from 1972 through 2000. The population of
international environmental treaties consists of thirty-eight treaties. The
variables chosen for inclusion in this analysis were selected based on a review of existing international relations theory and historical experiences of
states in the international environmental realm. The outcome variable for
this study is "the probability a state will become a party to an international
environmental treaty." In total, nine predictor variables were examined for
their influence on state behavior in the international environmental realm.

A binary dependent variable model of analysis (logit) was utilized in
this study. Despite the presence of some problems associated with using
logit in this context, this model was used because the resulting logit coefficients indicate whether a particular predictor variable would increase or
decrease the probability of the outcome variable. For that reason, the

analysis will focus on the interpretation of the correlation coefficients for the predictor variables.

Table 5.1 provides the summary statistics for the analyses that follows. It is now time to turn my attention to analyzing the correlation coefficients for each of the predictor variables.

THE PREDICTOR VARIABLES: INTERPRETATION OF CORRELATION COEFFICIENTS

Table 5.1 Logit Results for the Probability of a State Becoming a Party to an International Environmental Treaty

Dependent Variable: Probability a state will become a party to an international environmental treaty

Variable	Coefficient	Std. Error	z-Statistic	Prob.
International Environmental Treaty Type	0.265*	0.062	4.185	0.000
Impact on Military Interests of State	0.604*	0.057	10.426	0.000
Equitable Distribution of Treaty Costs	0.381*	0.058	6.569	0.000
Provision of Monitoring Mechanism	0.630*	0.066	9.518	0.000
Transfer of Technology	-0.108**	0.068	-1.596	0.110
Great Power Leadership	0.260*	0.068	3.853	0.000
Vulnerability to Environmental Problem	0.465*	0.041	11.315	0.000
Level of Freedom	0.243*	0.039	6.263	0.000
Gross National Product	0.250*	0.026	9.418	0.000

Note: N = 67998. The Log Likelihood Value is -6877.214. The probability levels for all variables except the "Impact on Military Interests of State are based on one-tailed tests. The probability level for the variable "Impact on Military Interests of the State" is based on a two-tail test. * Indicates that coefficient is significant at a .01 level of confidence. ** Indicates the coefficient is significant at a .10 level of confidence.

Environmental Treaty Type: Pollution Control versus Resource Management Treaties

It was originally proposed that international environmental treaty "type" was related to the probability of a state becoming a party to an international environmental treaty. To test this relationship, international environmental treaties included in this study were classified as being either pollution control or resource management treaties. Hypothesis 1 stated: *There is an increased probability that a state will become a party to an international environmental treaty if that treaty is a resource management treaty.* The underlying logic of this hypothesis was derived from the fact that pollution control treaties often entail additional costs that would place constraints on a state's economic competitiveness. For that reason, states are reluctant to become parties to such treaties despite a willingness to recognize the need for pollution control.

As shown in Table 5.1, there is a positive correlation of 0.265, statistically significant at the .01 level of confidence, between treaty type and becoming a party to an international environmental treaty. This finding indicates there is an increased probability that a state will become a party to a "resource management" treaty, thus supporting Hypothesis 1 and its underlying logic.

International Environmental Treaty's Impact on States' Military Interests

According to the neo-realist perspective, the most salient issues for states are those involving the military or national security. Given that the structure of the international system is characterized by anarchy, self-help, and the security dilemma, states seek to enhance their military position vis-à-vis other nation-states. Consequently, states are unlikely to engage in activities that threaten to compromise their military position or threaten their national security in the international arena. Following this logic, Hypothesis 2 stated: *There is a decreased probability that a state will become a party to an international environmental treaty if that treaty requires behavioral changes or imposes constraints on the military interests of the state.*

As shown in Table 5.1, the positive logit coefficient of 0.604, significant at the .01 level of confidence, challenges the above stated hypothesis. Rather, there appears to be an increased probability of a state becoming a party to such a treaty. This finding was totally unexpected and deserves a more comprehensive assessment.

In Chapter Six, then, I will explore the aforementioned relationship by conducting case studies on the five treaties identified as requiring behavioral changes or imposing constraints on the military interests of the state. These five treaties are: the *Convention on the Prohibition of the Development, Production and Stockpiling of Bacteriological (Biological) and Toxin Weapons, and on their Destruction (London, 1972); the Convention on the Prohibition of Military or Any Other Hostile Use of the Environmental Modification Techniques (Geneva, 1976); the Convention on the Physical Protection of Nuclear Material (Vienna, 1979); the Convention on Early Notification of a Nuclear Accident (Vienna, 1986); and, the Convention on Assistance in the Case of Nuclear Accident* (Vienna, 1986).

Equitable Distribution of Treaty Costs

Proposed solutions to environmental degradation are often constrained by the costs associated with employing new technologies. States are concerned with the fair allocation of these costs in order to prevent free-riding.[1] Therefore, relative gains concerns often impede cooperative undertakings. If a state concerned with equity issues can be guaranteed that the distribution of costs associated with an international environmental treaty are evenly dispersed among participants and that other states will behave according to the rules established in a cooperative agreement, there is an increased likelihood that cooperation will ensue. In other words, equitable burden sharing and increased transparency may foster cooperation. Classic equity issues, then, are likely to affect the probability a state will become a party to an international environmental treaty.

Three hypotheses were generated in order to test this proposition. The first hypothesis measures the direct effect of equity on the probability a state will become a party to an international environmental treaty: *Hypothesis 3—There is an increased probability that a state will become a party to an international environmental treaty if the costs associated with that treaty are equitably distributed among parties to the treaty; Hypothesis 4—There is a decreased probability that a state will become a party to an international environmental treaty if that treaty requires the state to transfer technology to another state; and, Hypothesis 5—There is an increased probability that a state will become a party to an international environmental treaty if that treaty provides mechanisms for monitoring state behavior.*

The positive logit coefficient for the variable "equitable distribution of treaty costs" (0.381), statistically significant at the .01 level of confidence, validates Hypothesis 3. In regard to technological transfers, Table 5.1 indicates a logit coefficient of -0.108, significant at a .10 level of confidence. Although not as significant as other findings in this study, the negative coefficient supports the assertion made in Hypothesis 4. As for the variable "monitoring mechanism," the positive logit coefficient of 0.630, again significant at the .01 level of confidence, substantiates Hypothesis 5.

Power Distribution in the International System

As discussed elsewhere in this study, power is a key concept in realist and neorealist explanations of international relations. Power not only determines the position of states within the international system; it ensures their survival within the system. Moreover, power defines the relationship between states. Power, as a variable, was used to measure whether or not more powerful states behave differently than less powerful states in the realm of international environmental politics.

The first area of analysis in regard to power distribution was the role of "great powers"[2] in the international environmental realm. Based on the assumption that "great powers" not only have the ability to influence the negotiation of international environmental treaties, they may also exert influence over less powerful states in the accession processes, the following hypothesis was tested: *Hypothesis 6—There is an increased probability that a state will become a party to an international environmental treaty if "great power(s)" assume a leadership role in the negotiation process of that treaty.*

As Table 5.1 shows, the logit coefficient for the variable "great power leadership" is 0.260, which is significant at the .01 confidence level. This finding supports the assertion made in Hypothesis 6. It seems reasonable to conclude, then, in the absence of great power leadership, there is a decreased probability a state will become a party to that treaty. But is that indeed the case? What happens when the great powers fail to reach consensus in regard to proposed solutions to an environmental problem? What affect does this have on the probability a state will become a party to an international environmental treaty? This question deserves further consideration. In Chapter VI, in addition to the aforementioned case studies, I will explore the ramifications of great power dissonance for participation in international environmental treaties using the *Convention on Biological Diversity* (1992), the negotiations of which were a source of discontent for at least one great power—the United States.

The second area of analysis involving the function of power in international environmental politics involves the role of GNP in a states' decision to become a party to an international environmental treaty. As discussed elsewhere, developed and developing states have long held varying viewpoints regarding the relationship between the environment and development.[3] Developing countries are far less likely to participate in international environmental treaties that place additional constraints on their ability to obtain higher levels of economic growth. For that reason, the following hypothesis was tested: *Hypothesis 7—There is an increased probability that a state will become a party to an international environmental treaty if the state has a high-income economy.*

As Table 5.1 reveals, "Gross National Product" is positively correlated to the probability of becoming a party to an international environmental treaty,[4] thus providing support for Hypothesis 7. This finding has important implications for the future of international environmental politics. The literature in the field suggests that states with prosperous economies and democratic political systems are better equipped to deal with the environmental problems confronting them. Prosperity, in particular, provides states with the necessary capabilities to advance their environmental concerns in the international system. Therefore, if a state is more likely to participate in an international environmental treaty as a condition of its economic well-being, one way in which to ensure environmental problems are adequately addressed is to promote economic growth and development. As states obtain higher levels of economic development, they will be able to acquire administrative systems capable of enacting environmental legislation and enforcing environmental controls.

Governmental Type

As previously mentioned, the literature on democracy, as well as international relations theory, suggest that states with more democratic forms of governance are better-equipped and more willing to deal with environmental problems. In an attempt to measure the influence of governmental type on state behavior in the environmental realm, a variable was created based upon levels of freedom.[5] The following hypothesis was tested: *Hypothesis 8—The greater level of freedom a state has, the more likely the state become a party to an international environmental treaty.*

The logit coefficient (0.243), significant at the .01 level of confidence, suggests that there is a positive relationship between governmental type and becoming a party to an international environmental treaty. If a state is more likely to participate in an international environmental treaty as a consequence of its level of freedom, one way in which to ensure environmental problems are adequately addressed is to promote democracy among states in the international system. In that way, as states obtain higher levels of freedom, they will become more responsive to public opinion, as well as the opinion of other states, while consolidating the necessary political institutions to advance environmental concerns both nationally and internationally.

This finding is extremely important. While the proposed relationship between democratic governmental types and pacific behavior is well established in the literature, similar discussions are absent from the literature on international environmental politics. Additionally, there have been few theoretical studies and empirical investigations pertaining to this relationship. Although preliminary in nature, this empirical investigation provides valuable insight into the relationship between governmental type and environmental behavior. Not only does this study provide empirical support for the propositions set forth in the literature, it expands the applicability of those propositions to the international environmental realm. This study also provides the groundwork for future studies.

Vulnerability to Environmental Problem

As discussed in Chapter Four of this study, the works of Volker von Prittwitz, Sprinz, Vaahtoranta; Repetto and Lash; and, Keohane and Nye all suggest that a state's willingness to engage in the creation and implementation of international environmental policy is directly related to the state's vulnerability to damage resulting from pollution.[6] A variable measuring "vulnerability" was created in order to determine whether or not a state's vulnerability to damage resulting from pollution or unsustainable resource management influences its decision to become a party to an international environmental treaty. The following hypothesis was tested in regard to ecological vulnerability: *Hypothesis 9—There is an increased probability that a state will become a party to an international environmental treaty if that state is more vulnerable to the particular environmental problem addressed in that treaty.* As shown in Table 5.1, the logit coefficient of 0.465, statistically significant at the .01 level of confidence, is consistent with the proposition set forth in Hypothesis 9.

PRELIMINARY CONCLUSIONS

Although this analysis was not as extensive as I would have liked it to have been, it did provide important insights into whether the predictor variables identified in this study affect the probability a state will become a party to an international environmental treaty.

What has been learned thus far? First, empirical evidence supports the proposition that states are more likely to become parties to international resource management treaties. Secondly, the evidence suggests that rather than decreasing the probability a state will become a party to an international environmental treaty, modification of military behavior actually increases the probability that a state would become a party to such a treaty. This finding will be further examined in Chapter VI. Third, the evidence suggests there is an increased probability of a state becoming a party to an international environmental treaty if: 1) the costs of adoption and implementation of a treaty are equitably distributed among the parties; 2) if the state is not required to transfer technology to another state; and, 3) if the treaty includes provisions for monitoring mechanisms. Fourth, we discovered the importance of great power leadership in the international environmental realm. Of particular importance was the realization that as states obtain higher levels of economic development they are more likely to become parties to international environmental treaties. As previously mentioned, the proposed relationship between democratic governmental types and international environmental behavior has been largely absent from the literature on international environmental politics. Although preliminary in nature, this empirical investigation provides valuable insight into this relationship. Finally, we discovered that the empirical evidence is consistent with the proposition that states more vulnerable to a particular environmental problem will be more likely to become a party to an international environmental treaty.

Before reaching any final conclusions regarding these findings, I would like to turn my attention to the case studies that follow. It is my hope that any additional information gleaned from these studies will help us understand more fully the applicability of international relations theory to international environmental politics.

Chapter Six

Becoming a Party to International Environmental Treaties: Case Studies

> An extraterrestrial observer might conclude that conversion of raw materials to wastes is the real purpose of human economic activity.

> —Gary Gardner & Paul Sampat (1999)

This chapter is devoted to exploring the questions raised in Chapter Five regarding state behavior and international environmental treaties. This chapter is divided into three sections. The first section will explore state behavior in regard to international environmental treaties with military implications. The second section explores the influence of great powers in the international environmental realm. The final section will be devoted to discussing the observations, which emerge from this undertaking.

INTERNATIONAL ENVIRONMENTAL TREATIES WITH MILITARY IMPLICATIONS

As discussed elsewhere, the neo-realist perspective asserts the most salient issues for states in the international system are those involving the military or national security. States seek survival in an international system characterized by anarchy, self-help, and the security dilemma. Therefore, states seek to enhance their military positions (thus ensuring survival and the protection of national interests) vis-à-vis other states in order to survive. From this logic is seemed reasonable to conclude states are unlikely to engage in activities that threaten to compromise their military position or threaten their national security in the international arena.

Hypothesis 2 of this study set out to test this proposition. Instead of confirming the relationship proposed by Hypothesis 2, the empirical evidence[1] suggested just the opposite was true of this relationship—there is an increased probability a state will become a party to an international environmental treaty if that treaty requires behavioral changes or imposes constraints on the military interests of the state. Given that this finding was unexpected, I decided to explore this relationship further by examining the five treaties identified as requiring behavioral changes or imposing constraints on the military interests of the state. These five treaties are: the *Convention on the Prohibition of the Development, Production and Stockpiling of Bacteriological (Biological) and Toxin Weapons, and on their Destruction* (London, 1972); the *Convention on the Prohibition of Military or Any Other Hostile Use of the Environmental Modification Techniques* (Geneva, 1976); the *Convention on the Physical Protection of Nuclear Material* (Vienna, 1979); the *Convention on Early Notification of a Nuclear Accident* (Vienna, 1986); and, the *Convention on Assistance in the Case of Nuclear Accident* (Vienna, 1986). By using the case study method to examine each of these treaties, it is my hope that I can glean a more fuller of understanding of those factors that influence state behavior in the international environmental realm.

Case Study #1: Convention on the Prohibition of the Development, Production and Stockpiling of Bacteriological (Biological) and Toxin Weapons, and on their Destruction *(London, 1972)*

The first treaty under consideration is the *Convention on the Prohibition of the Development, Production and Stockpiling of Bacteriological (Biological) and Toxin Weapons, and on their Destruction* (London, 1972).[2] This treaty has a direct affect on the military behavior of states because it prohibits the production and stockpiling of biological weapons. Since WWI, these weapons have been recognized for their enormous potential lethality because they lack discrimination in "whom" they kill.[3]

Although parties to the *Geneva Protocol* (1925) agreed not to use asphyxiating, poisonous, or other gases or biological weapons in war, pressures for even greater control measures arose for several reasons. First, numerous states (including the U.S.), had historically, not adhered to Geneva Convention.[4] Second, a number of countries retained huge stockpiles of both chemical and biological weapons. Third, scientific reports on the effects of possible biological weapons use were made increasingly available to both governments and the public in the 1960s.

In 1966, the "great powers" came under increasing pressure from the international community to reach an agreement on a treaty banning the production and stockpiling of bacteriological weapons.[5] An agreement was reached in 1971. The *Convention on the Prohibition of the Development,*

Production and Stockpiling of Bacteriological (Biological) and Toxin Weapons, and on their Destruction (London, 1972) was opened for signature in 1972. One hundred states, including all of the great powers, signed the treaty at this time.[6] This convention entered into force in 1975. Another twenty-four states became parties to this treaty between1973 and 2000, bringing the total number of parties to the treaty to one hundred and twenty four (124) states.

Table 6.1 Biological Weapons Status of States

Known/Former		Unknown/Suspected	
	Year became party		Year became party
Canada	1972	Algeria	—
Egypt	—	China	1984
France	1984	Cuba	1976
Germany	1972	Ethiopia	1975
India	1974	Italy	1975
Iran	1973	Myanmar	—
Iraq	1991	Pakistan	1974
Israel	—	South Korea	—
Japan	1982	Sudan	—
Libya	1982	Vietnam	1980
North Korea	—	Yugoslavia	—
Russia	1975		
South Africa	1975		
Syria	—		
Taiwan	1973		
United Kingdom	1975		
United States	1975		

Note: Data was collected from the Monterey Institute of International Studies "Center for Nonproliferation Studies;" Carnegie Endowment for International Peace "Nuclear Nonproliferation Project;" the US Arms Control and Disarmament Agency; the US Department of Defense; the Central Intelligence Agency; and, the International Institute for Strategic Studies; states were identified as either possessing or suspected of possessing biological weapons and/or capabilities. To determine whether or not these states became parties to the Convention on the Prohibition of the Development, Production and Stockpiling of Bacteriological (Biological) and Toxin Weapons, and on their Destruction, party information was collected from CEISIN Entri Thematic Guide and the United Nations Register of International Treaties and Other Agreements in the Field of the Environment (1997).

Upon examining the historical background of this treaty, it should be noted this treaty is first and foremost a treaty addressing military issues. Environmental considerations are of secondary importance to military concerns. In other words, this is not an international environmental treaty that requires modification of military behavior, but rather an international military treaty that has environmental implications. This, in and of itself, may be one reason why this particular treaty elicits a response from states other than the one expected.

Having said that, it does becomes clear that one factor that may have influenced states to become parties to this treaty was the role of the "great powers" (especially the United States and Soviet Union) in the negotiation process. Support for this assertion can be found in the work of Jacobson and Weiss, as well as Guruswamy.[7] Additional support comes from the empirical evidence presented in Chapter Five.

Another important factor that may have further induced states to become parties to this treaty was the climate of international relations at the time this treaty was negotiated. As Hurrell and Kingsbury observed,

> the overall climate of international relations affects the kinds of issues that find prominence on the international agenda. For instance, international concern for the environment in the early 1970s coincided with a period of détente between the USSR and the US.[8]

The fact that this treaty was negotiated during this same time period may be an important factor to consider when analyzing state behavior in regard to this treaty.

Although the evidence suggests that the provisions for monitoring mechanisms is positively correlated with an increased probability of states becoming parties to an international environmental treaty, this treaty contained no such provisions. It is important to consider the effect of such an absence on state behavior in regard to "military type" treaties. In the case of biological weapons, since the production of biological toxins can occur outside of military facilities, in such places as pharmaceutical or medical laboratories, the production of such toxins can be easily hidden from the "observant eye" of the international community. Due to the absence of inspection provisions, state compliance with the treaty cannot be verified. Therefore, a state may present itself as a reputable member of the international community by becoming a party to this treaty while "cheating" or engaging in the covert production and/or stockpiling of biological toxins. In this way, the state does not compromise its military position vis-à-vis other states. Table 6.1, above illustrates this phenomenon.

Two important observations emerged from this exercise. First, as Table 6.1 illustrates, although parties to this convention, the following countries remain suspected of engaging in the very behavior (developing, producing, and stockpiling) prohibited by the treaty: China, Cuba, Ethiopia, Italy, Pakistan, and Vietnam. Hence, the absence of monitoring mechanisms allowed countries, such as these, to become parties to the treaty while continuing to develop their biological weapons programs. So in reality, the treaty has no real impact on the military behavior of its parties. This point is reinforced by the second observation. Even though Iran and Iraq (both known biological weapons states) are parties to this treaty, they used these weapons against each other during the Iran-Iraq War of the 1980s. Furthermore, Iraq used biological weapons against its own people—the Kurds—at the end of the 1980s, and the possession of these weapons by Iraq during the *Gulf War* (1991) created the risk of them being used during the conflict. So even though known possessors of biological weapons and technology are parties to this treaty, the treaty does not preclude the use of such weapons and technology by parties to the treaty. The willingness (or increased probability) of states to become parties to these treaties may actually lie in the fact that without a mechanism through which to monitor their behavior, states can actually become parties to the treaty without having to modify their military behavior at all. Hence, a state's military position vis-à-vis other states is not necessarily compromised by such a treaty because: 1) the treaty does not preclude the use of such weapons; and, 2) the treaty does not provide appropriate oversight mechanisms to prevent the development, production and stockpiling of such weapons.

Case Study #2: Convention on the Prohibition of Military or Any Other Hostile Use of the Environmental Modification Techniques *(Geneva, 1976)*.

The second treaty that requires a state to alter its military behavior is the *Convention on the Prohibition of Military or Any Other Hostile Use of the Environmental Modification Techniques* (Geneva, 1976). Two of the earliest examples of the hostile use of environmental modification techniques occurred during World War II and the Korean War (1950–1953) when troops intentionally breached dams for the purpose of releasing contained waters on vulnerable troops and civilian populations.

However, it was not until after repeated attempts by the United States to modify the environment during the Second Indochina War (1961–1975)[9] that the Soviet Union initiated negotiations regarding the hostile use of environmental modification techniques. This convention prohibits its parties from engaging, among themselves, in the hostile use of techniques that would have widespread, long-lasting, or severe environmental effects as the means of damage.[10] Opened for signature in 1977, thirty-four states signed the convention. The convention entered into force on October 5, 1978, when the 20th state to sign the convention deposited its instrument of ratification. Between 1978 and 2000 another thirty-six states became parties to the convention, bringing the total number of parties to seventy states.

As in the case of the *Convention on the Prohibition of the Development, Production and Stockpiling of Bacteriological (Biological) and Toxin Weapons, and on their Destruction,* the evidence suggests that détente and/or "great power" leadership may have influenced a state's decision to become a party to this treaty. Furthermore, the lack of provisions requiring monitoring mechanisms may very well serve the same purpose they did in the aforementioned treaty—to allow states to become parties to the treaty without precluding the use of existing technology or the development of such technology for future use.

However, the work of Arthur Westing sheds additional light on another factor that should be taken into consideration[11]—the Lowest Common Denominator Effect. Westing acknowledges the importance of this treaty lies in the fact that it was one of the first treaties to incorporate environmental considerations into the law of war, but its weaknesses make it difficult to determine what military actions are prohibited:

> Not only would any actionable modifications have to have been admittedly (or somehow demonstrably) deliberate, they would additionally have to exceed in their environmental impact a threshold value that is defined in highly ambiguous terms (widespread, long-lasting, or severe). However, even if those terms had been rigorously defined by the treaty (which the negotiators refused to do), the very notion of a threshold value below which deliberate environmental modifications are permissible—a notion inserted at US insistence—thereby actually condones (and thus possibly even encourages) such actions up to some very ill defined level. The problem is that the ambiguities and other weaknesses of the existing body of law reflect precisely the extent to which the military powers of the world are to date willing to bend in these matters. [12]

Vague treaty language and concepts are often characteristic of treaties negotiated in the context of the "lowest common denominator" politics of international cooperation (LCD Effect). The LCD effect can be found when the process of decision-making involves multiple veto points or clearances.[13] The "LCD effect" results when states try to avoid collective action problems by using vague language and concepts or by designing compromises based on the demands of the least supportive party to a negotiation. In other words, by finding what is acceptable to the party most unwilling to bargain. This technique is often used in the negotiation of contentious issues to garner the support of a larger number of states. From Westing's analysis it seems reasonable to conclude that the negotiation of the *Convention on the Prohibition of Military or Any Other Hostile Use of the Environmental Modification Techniques* was a process characterized by the "LCD effect."

Case Studies #3–#5: Convention on the Physical Protection of Nuclear Material (Vienna, 1979), the Convention on Early Notification of a Nuclear Accident (Vienna, 1986), and the Convention on Assistance in the Case of a Nuclear Accident or Radiological Emergency (Vienna, 1986)

The last three treaties under consideration in this section have been grouped together because of their implications for the military behavior of states in the nuclear realm. These three treaties are the *Convention on the Physical Protection of Nuclear Material* (Vienna, 1979), the *Convention on Early Notification of a Nuclear Accident* (Vienna, 1986), and the *Convention on Assistance in the Case of a Nuclear Accident or Radiological Emergency* (Vienna, 1986).

Despite evidence of the international implications of the issue, there appears to have been no effective discussion of nuclear safety or waste disposal issues within the international community until the late 1970s. When the issue did reach the international agenda, countries with no nuclear industry tried to use the international system to impose stricter standards on neighboring countries that possessed such capabilities. The little international work that was done tended to be highly technical as illustrated by the *Convention on Liability in the Event of a Radiological Accident at Sea* (1971). Nuclear issues were conspicuously absent from the discussions that took place at the Stockholm Conference in 1972.

It was not until a series of nuclear accidents took place that the international community began to seriously address questions of nuclear safety and waste disposal. The *Convention on the Physical Protection of Nuclear Material* (Vienna, 1979) occurred at approximately the same time that a nuclear accident occurred at Three Mile Island in Pennsylvania. On April 26, 1986, a sequence of operator errors at the Chernobyl nuclear reactor, located in Ukraine, caused the worst civil nuclear accident in history. Twenty people were killed instantly. One hundred and sixteen thousand (116,000) people had to be immediately evacuated. A radioactive cloud spread across twenty-one states in West and Central Europe.

While there had been great difficulty in achieving international agreement on nuclear safety issues among members of the international community, this accident demonstrated the imperative political need to do so. Although there was a brief clash within Western Europe about where the work on a nuclear safety treaty should take place,[14] swift negotiations took place within the International Atomic Energy Agency (IAEA). The negotiations resulted in two treaties: *the Convention on Early Notification of a Nuclear Accident* (Vienna, 1986), and, the *Convention on Assistance in the Case of a Nuclear Accident or Radiological Emergency* (Vienna, 1986). Both of these treaties were negotiated within six months of the explosion. Also, both of them were signed by over seventy states and ratified by over forty countries by 2000.

In the above cases, it appears that the emergence of crises, rather than great power leadership, the "LCD effect," or other possible influences, were the most crucial factors leading to international action in regard to nuclear issues. As Karen Liftin notes,

> It may very well be the case that visibility may be crucial in order for an environmental disaster to inspire international regime building. The explosion in 1986 led to an update of the nuclear accident regime under the auspices of the International Atomic Energy Agency (IAEA)."[15]

Additional support for the conclusion that state participation in international environmental treaties may be disaster driven can be found in the following situations. Two giant oil spills in the late 1960s and one in the late 1970s,[16] led to the complete revision of the regimes governing marine pollution. Furthermore, the discovery of the ozone hole over Antarctica was a major factor determining the context and eventual outcome of the negotiations of the Montreal Protocol. Again, it appears that the international context in which negotiations of international environmental treaties occur is an important factor to take into consideration when considering state behavior in the environmental realm.

THE ROLE OF GREAT POWERS AND INTERNATIONAL ENVIRONMENTAL TREATIES

In exploring the relationship between power and a state's decision to become a party to an international environmental treaty, I decided to look at the influence of "great powers" in the international environmental realm. Literature in the field implies "great powers" not only have the ability to influence the negotiation of international environmental treaties, they may also exert influence over less powerful states in the processes. Hypothesis 6—*There is an increased probability that a state will become a party to an international environmental treaty with time if "great power(s)" assume a leadership role in the negotiation process of that treaty*—would test this proposition. The resulting correlation coefficient for the variable "great power leadership" (0.260) suggested the presence of great power leadership in the negotiation process increases the probability of a state becoming a party to an international environmental treaty with time. Therefore, it seemed reasonable to conclude the opposite effect—in the absence of great power leadership, there is a decreased probability a state will become a party to an international environmental treaty—would be true as well. But in order for either assertion to hold true, it must be assumed that the great powers have reached consensus on every international environmental problem and treaty being negotiated. History suggests that this is hardly the case. What happens, then, when the great powers fail to reach consensus in regard to proposed solutions to an environmental problem? What affect does this have on the probability a state will become a party to an international environmental treaty? I decided to explore these questions further.

The Convention on Biological Diversity (1992)

The *Convention on Biological Diversity* was one of two major treaties opened for signature at the United Nations Conference on Environment and Development (UNCED) in 1992. There were four principle objectives to the treaty: 1) it affirmed the sovereign rights of states over biological diversity found within their countries; 2) it deemed states responsible for conserving biological diversity within their territories; 3) the treaty directed states to use their biological diversity in a sustainable manner; and, 4) it promoted the fair and equitable sharing of the benefits arising out of the utilization of genetic resources, including by appropriate access to genetic resources and by the appropriate transfer of relevant technologies (taking into account all rights over those resources and to technologies) and by appropriate funding. The treaty entered into force in December 1993, after having received its thirtieth ratification in September of that same year. As of 2000, there were one hundred and seventy-five (175) parties, including the European Community, to the Convention on Biological Diversity.

The actual negotiations of the treaty can be traced to a 1987 UNEP decision to establish several ad hoc working groups of experts on biodiversity and biotechnology. By the sixth and what was to have been the last session of meetings, there were still major disagreements on most of the key issues. The principal provisions of the treaty went to the heart of sensitive land-use issues, biotechnology and sovereignty issues. Each party to the treaty was expected to establish conservation measures, including the designation of protected areas and restoration of degraded ecosystems. Political leaders were concerned with the economic implications of proposed changes in biological resource management. Although there appeared to be broad support, at least in principle, for the protection of threatened habitat and for the regulated use and collection of genetic materials, the commercial concerns about access to and property rights in species tended to drown out concerns about diversity and ecology.

Developing countries complained that many of their unique genetic resources were being exploited by biotechnology, agro-business and pharmaceutical companies headquartered in developed countries, which meant that little or no economic returns accrued to the host country. Even more problematic was that some of the genetically engineered products from this "exploitation" were allegedly sold at enormous profit by these firms to poor third world residents who were being asked to forego their own development in order to preserve the genetic base for such enterprises.

Representatives of biotechnology companies complained almost as bitterly about the efforts of the developing countries to undermine intellectual property rights with respect to plant and animal materials and to apply instead, self-serving notions of sovereign control over these living materials. The U.S. argued that biotechnology research and patents on gene stocks involved intellectual property rights which were owned by private companies and controlled by other international regimes, most notably the GATT. Japan and the U.S. also believed that regulation of biotechnology would stifle innovation. Led by the US negotiating team, opponents of the treaty insisted on rights to intellectual property not be overridden by provisions for country-of-origin protection and technology transfer requirements. They also insisted that the financing mechanisms for implementation of the treaty be changed to avoid explosive situations in which simple majority rule determined how much each donor country was obligated to pay. There was also disagreement as to whether to have global listings of key species and biological regions. The U.S., Canada, India, and Brazil opposed Japan, Australia, France, and several African countries on this issue.

The parties finally agreed that: 1) a state has the sovereign right to exploit its own resources; 2) the authority to determine access to genetic resources rests with national governments; and, 3) the benefits of research and development derived from biological resources taken from a developing country were expected to be made available to that country. The issues on global listings and finances were not resolved and the delegations agreed to meet one last time before UNCED. Agreement was finally reached at the last session on May 21, 1992. In the end, the opposition forces were unsuccessful in removing what they perceived as fatal flaws in treaty language, but only US refused to sign the convention.

If the assertions about the influence of "great powers" were correct, one might have assumed that the absence of participation by the US, the single remaining superpower, in this treaty would have led other great powers to distance themselves from the treaty as well. The US did privately urge other Western governments not to sign the treaty either, and indeed key Western states were anxiously evaluating the merits of participating in what appeared to be a defective treaty. There was little doubt that the views of the US were privately shared by a number of other Western leaders, evidence of which can be seen in the meager funding commitments that many of the wealthy nations made to implement both the treaty on climate change (also opened for signature at UNCED) and the treaty on biodiversity, as well as enact the hundreds of other provisions agreed to as part of Agenda 21.[17]

On the one hand, the weakness of the conservation obligations in the treaty and the ambiguity of its finance and technology provisions argued against signature. On the other hand, the agreement did constitute a minimal first step towards global action to tackle a recognized environmental threat. There were also serious political implications for the reputation of individual Western states of a decision not to sign the treaty. The US had not only isolated itself from its traditional allies, it cut itself off from other states around the globe. There were real political costs (both international and domestically) of being seen on the same side as the United States in this circumstance. In the case of the 1992 *Biodiversity Convention*, many negotiators from industrial states shared the US government's concerns about the treaty's provisions for intellectual property and financing mechanisms. But unlike the US, they chose to support the *Convention on Biological Diversity*. Calculating perhaps that the potential gains in cooperation and national prestige would more than offset the political and economic concessions implied by the treaty, all the major developed countries, except the US signed the treaty. It may just be the case that "a state's concern about its international image (e.g., avoidance of embarrassment) may be at least as important as its respect for international law, thus inviting grudging state participation in regimes that it does not truly favor."[18] So while the evidence suggests that great power leadership may increase the propensity of states becoming parties an international environmental treaty with time, the case of the biodiversity treaty illustrates that the influence may not rest in one great power alone.

As we saw in the *Convention on the Prohibition of the Development, Production and Stockpiling of Bacteriological (Biological) and Toxin*

Weapons, and on their Destruction (London, 1972) and the Convention on the Prohibition of Military or Any Other Hostile Use of the Environmental Modification Techniques (Geneva, 1976), this case study also suggests the presence of the "Least Common Denominator" Effect. Firm treaty commitments were thin. The actual negotiating process produced less willingness to compromise. The central issue facing states during negotiations was the insistence of the developing countries that they should get a more substantial return from Northern exploitation of Southern biodiversity. The North did not concede this, so the South (where most of the biodiversity is) was willing only to take on very limited conservation commitments.

Finally, the idea that the emergence of crises is often a crucial factor leading to international action receives further substantiation in the case of the Convention on Biodiversity. As discussed previously, the Torrey Canyon accident (March 1967), the oil explosion in the Santa Barbara Channel (1969) and the Amoco Cadiz oil spill (1978) led to the complete revision of the regimes governing marine pollution. The *Convention on the Physical Protection of Nuclear Material* (Vienna, 1979); the *Convention on Early Notification of a Nuclear Accident* (Vienna, 1986); and, the *Convention on Assistance in the Case of Nuclear Accident* (Vienna, 1986) had much the same effect, and led to an update of the nuclear accident regime under the auspices of the International Atomic Energy Agency (IAEA). Influential scientists had for years been arguing that the wholesale destruction of living species not only represented an irreversible squandering of the planet's genetic resources, it disrupted the ecological networks which human life might ultimately depend. International concern was growing as earlier policy initiatives had failed to slow down degradation. International concern for biodiversity was echoed in the popular environmental concerns of Western nations in the late 1980s. Therefore, scientific, popular and political concern about species destruction helped to create a perception of "biodiversity crises" at the time the *Convention on Biodiversity* was being negotiated.

CONCLUSIONS

In addition to the findings discussed in Chapter Five, the case studies performed in Chapter Six have provided additional insights into state behavior in the international environmental realm. First, understanding of great power leadership was expanded to include the realization that great power influence might not rest in one great power alone. Another important factor that came to light was the influence of the climate of international relations on states' decisions to become parties to international environmental accords. Third, it became apparent that the lack of provisions requiring monitoring mechanisms might allow states to become parties to an international environmental treaty without having to modify their behavior at all. Fourth, the case studies revealed the importance of considering the "Lowest Common Denominator" Effect when evaluating the probability a state would become a party to an international environmental treaty. Finally, the case studies supported the proposition that the emergence of crises is crucial to international environmental action.

Given that a great deal of information regarding state behavior in regard to international environmental treaties has been collected in Chapter Five and Chapter Six, it is now time to turn my attention to the importance of these findings for international relations theory and its applicability to the international environmental realm.

Chapter Seven
Conclusions

> The core of the problem of how to achieve results from cooperation is that trail and error in learning is slow and painful . . . perhaps if we understand the process better we can use our foresight to speed up the evolution of cooperation.
>
> —Robert Axelrod (1990) *The Evolution of Cooperation,* p. 191.

The conclusions drawn from this study are divided into two sections. The first section examines the ability of international relations theory to explain state behavior in the international environmental realm. The second section provides summary conclusions as well as discusses the contributions of this study to the field of international relations.

THEORY AND PRACTICE: INTERNATIONAL RELATIONS THEORY AND EXPLANATIONS OF STATE BEHAVIOR IN THE INTERNATIONAL ENVIRONMENTAL REALM

The purpose of this study was to evaluate the applicability of international relations theory to international environmental politics. The predictor variables selected for the empirical analyses were created based on their ability to correspond to underlying assumptions of existing international relations theories, as well as the historical experiences of states in the international environmental realm. Case studies were not only conducted for the purpose of applying the empirical findings, but to further examine unexpected behaviors by states in the international environment. Based on these findings, it is now time to examine the relationship between international relations theory and explanations of state behavior in the international environmental realm to determine if there is indeed the lack of a single comprehensive theory that can address the range of complex processes and factors which have been shown to influence state behavior in the international system and the international environment.

International Environmental Politics

The literature on international environmental politics has been traditionally focused on the examination of regimes, institutions, and international laws. There has been a tremendous amount of knowledge gained through these examinations as well as studies that have examined the roles of NGOs, epistemic communities, and other non-state actors in the formulation of international environmental policy. Therefore, existing approaches to the study of international environmental politics do not need to be swept aside. To do so would be a great waste.

However, the existing approaches should be recognized for what they are: policy-oriented methods of inquiry and explanations with a relatively narrow focus. In other words, international environmental politics literature has been too narrowly focused on the question of what makes cooperation feasible or not. In the process, the literature has ignored what has been taking place in the broader realm of international relations. It has overlooked the existing assumptions and foundations of International Relations theory. With this in mind, these types of approaches should not be used without acknowledging the broader contexts of which they are a part. Better yet, what has been gained from the approaches used in international environmental politics should be merged into a more comprehensive framework of analysis that permits a broader understanding of events and interactions. To do this, one must look to international relations theory.

Theories of International Relations

Theories of Social Construction

Although it was not my original intent to test the underlying assumptions of social constructivism, the findings revealed in the case studies pertaining to "crises" and the "perception of crises," in addition to the empirical findings regarding "vulnerability," required I reevaluate the usefulness of this body of theory in explaining state behavior in the international environmental realm for possible inclusion in a broader explanatory framework.

Returning to the previous discussion of this theory in Chapter Two, social construction theorists assert that different people and groups construct their understanding of the global environment in different ways. This in turn leads to different assumptions and perceptions of environmental needs and different understandings of global environmental interdependence. Therefore, the perception of the environmental problem in question may influence state behavior in the international environmental realm—the greater the perception of ecological calamity, the more likely a state will become a party to a specified international environmental treaty with time.

As the case studies on the *Convention on the Physical Protection of Nuclear Material* (Vienna, 1979); the *Convention on Early Notification of a Nuclear Accident* (Vienna, 1986); the *Convention on Assistance in the Case of Nuclear Accident* (Vienna, 1986) revealed, crises and resulting perceptions of vulnerability compelled states to become parties to the aforementioned treaties. In the case of the *Convention on Biodiversity* (1992) the perception of a crisis of biodiversity seemed to elicit a similar response from states in the international community. Finally, the positive correlation coefficient associated with the variable "vulnerability" indicated that states are more likely to become parties to international environmental treaties as a result of their vulnerability or exposure to an international environmental problem.

Certainly there are concrete factors that can be used to determine a state's vulnerability to an environmental problem (e.g., coastal states are more vulnerable to the effects of global warming than non-coastal states due to the accompanying increases in sea-level). On the other hand, vulnerability may very well be defined by a state's views or opinions of situations and circumstances, thus perceptional. Therefore, an environmental threat, whether real or imagined, can compel a state to take action in order to protect itself and survive. Although emanating from social construction theory, this insight is at the core of structural explanations of state behavior in the international system, and will be returned to later in this chapter.

Liberalism

Liberal explanations of state behavior in the international system are contingent upon the existence of international organizations (IOs) and regimes, democracy, and markets. In regard to international organizations and regimes, the liberal approach specifies a prominent role for governments and international organizations (IOs) in the international environment. Liberalism maintains that national governments and IOs are essential to international environmental governance in an international system characterized by anarchy. This theoretical framework has shown how cooperation has been facilitated through international institutions and their mechanisms for generating consensus, norms, laws, and enforcement procedures.

Additionally, liberalism suggests that environmental behavior is linked to economic considerations and democracy. Liberalism asserts that states with prosperous economies and more free and open systems of government are better equipped to face the environmental problems confronting them. In regard to economic considerations, the liberal position relies heavily on the idea that the best way to protect the global commons is to privatize it. Liberalism believes there must be an effective equilibrium between the demand of economic development and environmental protection by bringing market forces to bear upon both interests. Liberals are wary of environmental regulations that curb market forces or stress the role of the state. They argue that state control over industries and extensive regulation of the environment will not produce desirable environmental and economic outcomes. Additionally, the price signals provided by free markets have produced a much less wasteful and environmentally destructive allocation of resources than has been achieved in circumstances where they have not been available. (e.g., world's agricultural markets)

Liberalism also asserts that the impulse for environmental protection is very much a democratic phenomenon. Democracy provides channels[1] for public and consumer pressure that is necessary to counterbalance the producer pressure which typically dominates governmental decision-making and which tends to be deployed in opposition to environmental regulation. These freedoms have been available in that part of the world where environmental protection has gone the furthest—the democracies of the West. Where these freedoms have been absent, it has been impossible for popular concern about environmental degradation to exert effective pressure upon the authorities. Those authorities have shown little concern for the environment in the absence of such pressure. Given numerous examples where authoritarianism and government suppression of market signals have damaged the environment,[2] it is difficult not to conclude that the best way to protect the environment is a through the maintenance of individual political and economic freedoms.

In sum, the distinguishing features of the liberal view of environmental protection are the prominent roles of international organizations, democracy, and markets. The empirical evidence presented in this study lends support to the liberal world-view. First, the evidence reveals the importance of monitoring mechanisms for increasing the probability a state becomes a party to an international environmental treaty with time. Secondly, the evidence does suggest a link between the economy and democracy. In regard to the economy, the evidence shows an increased probability states will become parties to international environmental treaties as they experience increased levels of economic growth. Once individuals have achieved a certain level of material affluence, they turn their attention from meeting immediate needs to long-term needs, which include environmental considerations. Moreover, as countries become richer they acquire the administrative systems to enforce environmental controls and thus protect the common good against individual self-interest. In the developing world, the absence of prosperity has produced resistance to agreements that are seen as constraining prospects for economic growth. Weak administrative infrastructures, also characteristic of this part of the world, inhibit the ability of developing states to enforce environmental laws they have introduced. Growth and development today occur within the context of the international liberal economy. As to democracy, the evidence clearly suggests that as states acquire greater levels of freedom, they are more likely to become parties to international environmental treaties. These two findings have important ramifications for international environmental politics. Specifically, if economic growth and democratic forms of governance are related to increased participation in the international environmental realm, then efforts to reduce environmental degradation should include policies which foster growth and liberalization of political systems.

Realism and Its Variants

Over the objections of some international relations scholars, realism and its modified versions do provide useful insights regarding state behavior in the international environmental realm. The contributions of the structural realist framework to international environmental politics are rather similar to its contributions to International Relations theory and essentially to the understanding of how and why the international system operates as it does. The traditional realist literature has helped explain why states have resisted cooperation in the past, why they often continue to resist cooperation in the current system, and why they often resist the adoption of environmental policies that benefit themselves as well as other states.

According to realism, states should be kept abreast of potential environmental threats, but they should not sacrifice more important and more immediate interests such as stable and diversified economies or strong military capabilities.[3] Realists argue that free riding on any global agreement would be quite easy and highly likely. While many, if not most states are willing to cooperate in curbing environmental degradation, other states, free-riders, can reap the rewards of environmental improvement without paying the price. Free-riding states can then devote their resources to increasing their economic or military strength at the expense of the environment and collective efforts of states to reduce degradation. Free-riding states can nullify efforts to check environmental degradation. The end result is similar to the prisoner's dilemma. If everyone cooperates, the efforts to curb environmental degradation are likely to be effective, producing the best outcome for all states across the planet. Unfortunately, the incentives to defect loom large. If one large polluter, such as the US or China, defects or if a group of states defect, efforts to stop environmental degradation by other states are for nothing. For this reason, each state is better off not cooperating because chances are high some state is going to defect.

Which states are likely to be free-riders? Realists in the North argue that developing states are more likely to free-ride because they can carry on with their business (e.g., economic development at the cost of environmental degradation) as usual while the North is not only expected to transform their way of life (e.g., reduce pollution), but pay for the cost of implementation and compliance of international environmental accords in the South. The advanced industrialized states of the North would be foolish to agree to such costly and substantive changes amidst reticence from the South to comply. Realists from the developing world take another view entirely. They argue that environmental degradation is the fault of advanced industrial powers whose status is directly related to their long history of environmental degradation. And yet, advanced industrialized states want to distribute the cost of environmental degradation onto developing countries—costs they cannot afford. The only issue the North and South agree upon in matters pertaining to the environment is the loss of state sovereignty—neither is willing to experience such a loss. Therefore, the best that can be expected from states in the absence of a higher authority is to tend to their own economic and security needs and respond to environmental threats when those problems do not impinge upon economic or security concerns, or infringe upon the national interests of the state.

Although this study did not directly address the issue of free-riding, there is empirical evidence which might be interpreted as supporting realist assertions that states should not sacrifice more important and more immediate interests such as stable and diversified economies or strong military capabilities to environmental concerns. As the evidence regarding "treaty type" suggests, states are more likely to become parties to international resource management treaties than pollution control treaties. This behavior is directly related to the fact that the costs of pollution control treaties often constrain the economic competitiveness of states in the international trading system. Constraints on a state's economy can hamper its ability to reach higher levels of economic development, thus preventing it from attaining increased levels of power in the international system. Economic constraints can also prevent states from maintaining their current economic and power position in the international system. Furthermore, if one state's economy is constrained by an agreement, while another state is not, one state may economically gain at the expense of other states, with the potential of that gain being used to enhance one state's position in the international system vis-à-vis other states.

Secondly, the evidence suggests that there is an increased probability that states will become parties to international environmental treaties when the costs associated with the adoption and implementation of those treaties is equally distributed among the parties. Inequitable distribution of such costs not only invites free-riding, it increases the security dilemma more generally.[4] The same can be said for the issue of technological transfers. While provisions for monitoring mechanisms may alleviate some of those concerns, the presence of such mechanisms does not preclude states from engaging in the activities prohibited by the treaty. So long as there is no adjudication, compliance cannot be guaranteed.

Another assumption of realism is that states will not engage in activities that require them to compromise their military strength. Consequently, it was proposed that there would be a decreased probability of states becoming parties to international environmental treaties that required the modification of military behavior with time. On the surface, the empirical evidence appeared to challenge this assumption—calling into question the very essence of realism itself. But, a more in depth analysis carried out through the case study method, revealed that a state could become a party to such a treaty and not compromise its military position unless it chose to do so. In that way, states can present the image of a credible player without forgoing national security concerns.

The evidence presented in this study also suggests that power matters—a central assumption of structural realism. Neo- or structural realism asserts that state behavior is motivated by the need to maintain its power position in the international system in order to survive. Power differentials are illustrated by the classification of states into categories reflecting income levels based on gross national product. Great powers have high levels of economic development usually accompanied by great military strength. As a result of having more power than other members of the international community, great powers not only have increased capabilities to address environmental concerns, they have the ability to exert influence over other states as well as over the negotiation of international accords. As the evidence suggests, the presence of great powers can compel states to become parties to international environmental treaties. Therefore, it seems reasonable to conclude that influence can be used to advance a state's national interest by influencing policy outcomes.

Power is also central to any discussion of the North-South environmental divide. The North consists of the advanced industrial states with high-income economies. The South, on the other hand, is made up states in the process of developing, thereby categorized as low—to middle- income economies. This so called divide between the "have's" and "have not's" has been characteristic of international environmental politics since before Stockholm in 1972. The states of the South have long maintained the need for economic development even if it meant sacrificing the environment. Furthermore, there is no reason believe that governments in the developing world will abandon their efforts to achieve higher levels of economic development soon. The empirical results of this study seem to indicate that as countries prosper they will devote more attention to environmental problems because they have the power capabilities to do so. In order for states to economically develop, they will need assistance from the international community. But as we have seen, any collective action on this front will have to be achieved with little or no net loss in a participating nation's economic competitiveness, which does not beckon well for future economic development in the South. Finally, neorealism is supported by the observation that the structure of the international system at the time of the treaty's negotiation may influence a state's decision to become a party to that treaty.

When looking at realism and its modified versions for explanations of state behavior in the international environmental realm, one must also take into account the "Least Common Denominator" Effect. Given the existence of relative gains concerns, in addition to the various interests of states, not to mention the sheer number of states involved in the negotiation process, it is a wonder that cooperation is achieved at all. Therefore, it should be no surprise that in order to garner the greatest support for an international environmental policy, states often adopt compromises based on the demands of the least supportive party to a negotiation. Although the LCD may encourage states to become parties to international environmental treaties, it dilutes the influence of the overall treaty.

Finally, while it may be inferred from the evidence presented in this study that a state's national interest influences it decision to become a party to an international environmental treaty, an inference supported in much of the literature, this study cannot directly confirm this assertion. No variable was created and no data was collected that would directly measure the influence of national interest. This question will have to be left for future studies.

SUMMARY CONCLUSIONS

This study was meant to provide the groundwork for more comprehensive investigations into the question of whether international relations theory could explain state behavior in the international environmental realm. Specifically, I examined state behavior in regard to them becoming parties to international environmental treaties. The importance of this question lies in fact that as international environmental treaties have become the main tool through which states in the international system address environmental concerns, identification of those factors that enhance the likelihood of participation will allow for their inclusion in future negotiations and thus ensure a better record of participation to international environmental treaties in the future.

The findings of this study did reveal several factors that were related to the increased probability of a state becoming a party to an international environmental treaty with time. These factors included: treaty type (with international resource management treaties increasing the probability of state participation with time); the modification of military behavior; the equitable distribution of treaty costs; the presence of monitoring mechanisms; the presence of great power leadership; higher levels of economic development coupled with greater levels of freedom; and, increase vulnerability to an environmental problem. This study also revealed that international environmental treaties that required one state or group of states to transfer technology to another state(s) would decrease the probability of state participation with time.

Case studies were also conducted. These cases studies revealed additional factors that influence state participation. These factors include: the structure of the international system at the time the treaties were negotiated; the perception of environmental crises; and, the "Least Common Denominator" Effect.

These variables were then examined within the context of international relations theory in order to determine if international relations theory can explain state behavior in the environmental realm, and whether creating a more comprehensive theory is warranted. First, and foremost, international relations theory proves quite capable of explaining state behavior in regard to international environmental treaties as well as international environmental politics.

In fact, by drawing on the variants of international relations theory, one can arrive at a comprehensive explanation of state behavior in the environmental realm. Therefore, it seems reasonable to conclude that international environmental politics can be studied within the broader international relations framework.

On a final note, this study has led to the recognition that environmental issues have escaped from the domain of domestic politics. In fact, they have escaped from the even larger domain of international environmental politics. Environmental issues have now invaded the domain of every area of international relations and are continuing to do so with growing speed. Environmental issues have penetrated all aspects of the international political economy, from trade and finance to development politics (especially North-South economic relations) to national and international systems of accounts (e.g., challenging the measurements of GNP and the like). Additionally, environmental issues have begun to penetrate nearly all aspects of security and conflict issues. Environmental problems are of the roots of conflict. The resolution of these conflicts is often the means of providing national and international security. When such fundamental changes take place in the international system, we know, from theories and practice, that the ramifications can be universally profound.

As evidenced in this study, leadership in the international environmental realm is one way to meet the growing challenges posed by the international environment. While the ability to influence state behavior in the environmental realm might not rest in one "great power" alone, a powerful state not only has the ability to influence the negotiation of international environmental treaties, they may also exert influence over less powerful states in the process. By 1993, not only had a growing number of states declared their support for "values consistent with American ideals"[5] (including the preservation of the global environment), the opportunity for leadership in the international environmental realm fell to the United States who had by this time achieved unparalleled international influence and authority. As Richard H. Stanley noted:

> the United States is better placed than any other nation to exercise genuine world leadership. With the ending of the East-West divide which dominated international politics for most of the last half century, this country emerged as the sole remaining superpower.[6]

But despite the Clinton administration's commitment to protect the international environment, failure to muster the necessary support for such an agenda from the Republican dominated Congress prevented the United States from providing leadership in the international environmental realm. Any hopes of the United States changing course were dashed with the election of George W. Bush to the presidency of the United States in 2000. As discussed elsewhere in this book, during the first two years in office the Bush administration compiled "the most anti-environmental record of an US president in history.[7] Obviously, the United States has chosen not to lead the international community toward a new international environmental agenda in the immediate post-Cold War era.

In the absence of "great power" leadership and in an international community faced by challenges to multilateralism posed by the growing preferences among state governments and non-state actors for "unilateralism and coalitions-of-the willing,"[8] the United Nations Environmental Programme stepped forward at the *World Summit on Sustainable Development* (August 26—September 4, 2002) to assume leadership in the international environmental realm. At this summit, UNEP declared:

> We reaffirm our commitment to the principles and purposes of the UN Charter and international law as well as the strengthening of multilateralism. We support the leadership role of the United Nations as the most universal and representative organization in the world, which is best placed to promote sustainable development.[9]

Although UNEP receives funding in the form of a contribution from the United Nations Regular Budget, most of its environmental work depends entirely on voluntary support of the Environmental Fund.[10] However, "contributions to the Environment Fund continue to fall short of the budget approved by UNEP's Governing Council, forcing UNEP to scale down its work programme.[11] Although willing to assume this leadership role, UNEP will not be able to secure the future of the international environment unless the international community of states is willing to provide it with the funds and resources it needs. The future of the environment, then, hangs in the balance.

Appendix A
International Environmental Treaties 1972–1997

Convention for the Conservation of Antarctic Seals, London, 1972

Convention on the Prohibition of the Development, Production and Stockpiling of Bacteriological (Biological) and Toxin Weapons, and on Their Destruction, London, Moscow, Washington, 1972

Convention Concerning the Protection of the World Cultural and Natural Heritage, Paris, 1972

Convention on the Prevention of Marine Pollution by Dumping of Wastes and Other Matter (as amended), London, Mexico City, Moscow, [Washington], 1972

Protocol Relating to Intervention on the High Seas in Cases of Marine Pollution by Substances Other than Oil, London, 1973

Convention on International Trade in Endangered Species of Wild Fauna and Flora, Washington, 1973

International Convention for the Prevention of Pollution from Ships, London, 1973

Convention Concerning Prevention and Control of Occupational Hazards Caused by Carcinogenic Substances and Agents, Geneva, 1974

Convention on the Prohibition of Military or Any Other Hostile Use of Environmental Modification Techniques, Geneva, 1976

Convention Concerning the Protection of Workers Against Occupational Hazards in the Working Environment Due to Air Pollution, Noise and Vibration, Geneva, 1977

Protocol of 1978 Relating to the International Convention for the Prevention of Pollution from Ships, London, 1973

International Plant Protection Convention, Rome, 1951 1979

Convention on the Conservation of Migratory Species of Wild Animals, Bonn, 1979

Convention on the Physical Protection of Nuclear Material, Vienna, 1979

Convention on the Conservation of Antarctic Marine Living Resources, Canberra, 1980

Convention Concerning Occupational Safety and Health and the Working Environment, Geneva, 1981

Protocol to Amend the Convention on Wetlands of International Importance Especially as Waterfowl Habitat, Paris, 1982

United Nations Convention on the Law of the Sea, Montego Bay, 1982

International Tropical Timber Agreement, Geneva, 1983

Vienna Convention for the Protection of the Ozone Layer, Vienna, 1985

Convention Concerning Occupational Health Services, Geneva, 1985

Convention Concerning Safety in the Use of Asbestos, Geneva, 1986

Convention on Early Notification of a Nuclear Accident, Vienna, 1986

Convention on Assistance in the Case of a Nuclear Accident or Radiological Emergency, Vienna, 1986

United Nations Convention on Conditions for the Registration of Ships, Geneva, 1986

Montreal Protocol on Substances that Deplete the Ozone Layer, Montreal, 1987

Convention on the Regulation of Antarctic Mineral Resource Activities, Wellington, 1988

Basel Convention on the Control of Transboundary Movements of Hazardous Wastes and Their Disposal, Basel, 1989

International Convention on Salvage, London, 1989

Convention on Civil Liability for Damage Caused During Carriage of Dangerous Goods by Road, Rail and Inland Navigation Vessels, Geneva, 1989

London Amendment to the Montreal Protocol on Substances that Deplete the Ozone Layer, London, 1990

Convention Concerning Safety in the Use of Chemicals at Work, Geneva, 1990

International Convention on Oil Pollution Preparedness, Response and Cooperation, London, 1990

Protocol to the Antarctic Treaty on Environmental Protection, Madrid, 1991

United Nations Framework Convention on Climate Change, New York, 1992

Convention on Biological Diversity, Rio de Janeiro, 1992

United Nations Convention of Desertification, Paris, 1994

Kyoto Protocol, Kyoto, 1997

Appendix B

Nation-State Data: Year of Entry into International System, Year in Which Population Reaches 1 Million, and Years Included in This Study

	year of entry into international system	year in which Population reaches 1 million	years included in this study
Afghanistan	1920	1942	1972–2000
Albania	1914–1939; 1944	1942	1972–2000
Algeria	1962	1965	1972–2000
Angola	1975	1970	1975–2000
Argentina	1841	1942	1972–2000
Armenia	1991	1990	1991–2000
Australia	1920	1942	1972–2000
Austria	1919–1938; 1955	1950	1972–2000
Azerbaijan	1991	1990	1991–2000
Bangladesh	1972	1970	1972–2000
Belarus	1991	1990	1991–2000
Belgium	1830–1940; 1945	1942	1972–2000
Benin	1960	1950	1972–2000
Bhutan	1971	1990	1990–2000
Bolivia	1848	1942	1972–2000
Bosnia & Herzegovina	1992	1990	1992–2000
Botswana	1966	1990	1990–2000

	year of entry into international system	year in which Population reaches 1 million	years included in this study
Brazil	1826	1942	1972–2000
Bulgaria	1908	1942	1972–2000
Burkina Faso	1960	1950	1972–2000
Burundi	1962	1950	1972–2000
Cambodia	1953	1950	1972–2000
Cameroon	1960	1950	1972–2000
Canada	1920	1942	1972–2000
Central African Republic	1960	1950	1972–2000
Chad	1960	1950	1972–2000
Chile	1839	1942	1972–2000
China	1860	1942	1972–2000
Colombia	1831	1942	1972–2000
Congo	1960	1965	1972–2000
Costa Rica	1920	1965	1972–2000
Cote d'Ivoire	1960	1950	1972–2000
Croatia	1992	1990	1992–2000
Cuba	1909	1942	1972–2000
Czechoslovakia	1918–39/1945–92	1942	1972–2000
Denmark	1816–1940; 1945	1942	1972–2000
Dominican Republic	1925	1942	1972–2000
Ecuador	1854	1942	1972–2000
Egypt	1937	1942	1972–2000
El Salvador	1875	1950	1972–2000
Estonia	1918–1940; 1991	1950	1991–2000
Ethiopia	1898–1936; 1941	1950	1972–2000
Finland	1917	1942	1972–2000
France	1816–1942; 1944	1942	1972–2000
Gabon	1960	1990	1990–2000
Georgia	1991	1990	1991–2000
Germany, FR	1955–90	1950	1972–2000
Germany, DR	1954–90	1950	1972–2000
Germany	1990	1990	1990–2000
Ghana	1957	1950	1972–2000

	year of entry into international system	year in which Population reaches 1 million	years included in this study
Greece	1828–1941; 1944	1942	1972–2000
Guatemala	1868	1950	1972–2000
Guinea	1958	1950	1972–2000
Guinea-Bissau	1974	1995	1974–2000
Haiti	1934	1942	1972–2000
Honduras	1899	1950	1972–2000
Hungary	1919	1950	1972–2000
India	1947	1942	1972–2000
Indonesia	1949	1950	1972–2000
Iran	1855	1942	1972–2000
Iraq	1932	1942	1972–2000
Israel	1948	1950	1972–2000
Italy	1816	1942	1972–2000
Jamaica	1962	1942	1972–2000
Japan	1860–1945; 1952	1942	1972–2000
Jordan	1946	1950	1972–2000
Kazakhstan	1991	1990	1991–2000
Kenya	1963	1950	1972–2000
Korea, DPR	1948	1942	1972–2000
Korea, Rep	1949	1942	1972–2000
Kuwait	1961	1990	1990–2000
Kyrgyzstan	1991	1990	1991–2000
Laos	1954	1950	1972–2000
Latvia	1918–1940; 1991	1950	1991–2000
Lebanon	1946	1950	1972–2000
Lesotho	1966	1990	1990–2000
Liberia	1920	1965	1972–2000
Libya	1952	1950	1972–2000
Lithuania	1918–1940; 1991	1950	1991–2000
Madagascar	1960	1950	1972–2000
Malawi	1964	1950	1972–2000
Malaysia	1957	1950	1972–2000
Mali	1960	1950	1972–2000
Mauritania	1960	1965	1972–2000

	year of entry into international system	year in which Population reaches 1 million	years included in this study
Mauritius	1968	1990	1990–2000
Mexico	1831	1942	1972–2000
Moldova	1991	1990	1991–2000
Mongolia	1921	1965	1972–2000
Morocco	1956	1942	1972–2000
Mozambique	1975	1970	1975–2000
Myanmar	1948	1942	1972–2000
Namibia	1990	1990	1990–2000
Nepal	1920	1942	1972–2000
Netherlands	1816–1940;1945	1942	1972–2000
New Zealand	1920	1942	1972–2000
Nicaragua	1900	1942	1972–2000
Niger	1960	1950	1972–2000
Nigeria	1960	1950	1972–2000
Norway	1905–40;1945	1942	1972–2000
Oman	1971	1990	1990–2000
Pakistan	1947	1950	1972–2000
Panama	1920	1965	1972–2000
Papua New Guinea	1975	1970	1975–2000
Paraguay	1846	1950	1972–2000
Peru	1839	1942	1972–2000
Philippines	1946	1942	1972–2000
Poland	1919–39;1945	1942	1972–2000
Portugal	1816	1942	1972–2000
Romania	1878	1942	1972–2000
Russian Fed	1989	1980	1989–2000
Rwanda	1962	1950	1972–2000
Saudi Arabia	1927	1950	1972–2000
Senegal	1960	1950	1972–2000
Sierra Leone	1961	1950	1972–2000
Singapore	1965	1965	1972–2000
Slovenia	1992	1990	1992–2000
Somalia	1960	1950	1972–2000
South Africa	1920	1942	1972–2000

	year of entry into international system	year in which Population reaches 1 million	years included in this study
Spain	1816	1942	1972–2000
Sri Lanka (Ceylon)	1948	1950	1972–2000
Sudan	1956	1950	1972–2000
Sweden	1816	1942	1972–2000
Switzerland	1816	1942	1972–2000
Syria	1946–58;1961	1950	1972–2000
Taiwan	1949	1950	1972–2000
Tajikistan	1991	1990	1991–2000
Tanzania	1961	1950	1972–2000
Thailand	1887	1942	1972–2000
Togo	1960	1950	1972–2000
Trinidad & Tobago	1962	1990	1990–2000
Tunisia	1956	1950	1972–2000
Turkey	1816	1942	1972–2000
Turkmenia	1991	1990	1991–2000
Uganda	1962	1950	1972–2000
Ukraine	1991	1980	1991–2000
UAE	1971	1990	1990–2000
United Kingdom	1818	1942	1972–2000
United States	1816	1920	1972–2000
USSR	1921–1989	1942	1972–2000
Uruguay	1882	1942	1972–2000
Uzbekistan	1991	1990	1991–2000
Venezuela	1841	1942	1972–2000
Vietnam, DR	1954	1950	1972–2000
Vietnam, Rep	1954–1975	1950	1972–2000
Yemen	1926	1950	1972–2000
Yugoslavia	1878–1941; 1944–1992	1942	1972–2000
Zaire	1960	1950	1972–2000
Zambia	1964	1950	1972–2000
Zimbabwe	1966	1966	1972–2000

Appendix C
Nuclear Status of Nation-States, 1999[*]

Declared Nuclear-Weapon Nation-States: China, France, Russia, United Kingdom, and United States.

Soviet Successor Nation-States with Nuclear Weapons on Territory: Belarus, Ukraine, and Kazakhstan.

Undeclared Nuclear-Weapon Nation-States: India, Israel, and Pakistan.

Active/Suspected Nuclear-Weapons Program: Iran, Libya, and North Korea.

Recent Renunciations: Algeria, Argentina, Brazil, Iraq, Romania, and South Africa.

Nation-States with the Technical Capacity to Operate Nuclear Weapons or Possess Stocks of Weapon-Usable Nuclear Material: Australia, Austria, Belgium, Canada, the Czech Republic, Denmark, Finland, Germany, Hungary, Ireland, Italy, Japan, Netherlands, Norway, Poland, Slovakia, South Korea, and Spain.

[*] Information provided by the Nuclear Non-Proliferation Project, Carnegie Endowment for International Peace.

Appendix D
Biological Weapons Status
of Nation-States[*]

Unknown/Suspected: Algeria, China, Cuba, Ethiopia, Italy, Myanmar, Pakistan, South Korea, Sudan, Vietnam, Yugoslavia

Known/Former: Canada, Egypt, France, Germany, India, Iran, Iraq, Israel, Japan, Libya, North Korea, Russia, South Africa, Syria, Taiwan, United Kingdom, United States

[*] Information provided by the "Center for Nonproliferation Studies."

Classification of Regions

EAST ASIA AND PACIFIC (1)

Laos	Philippines	Cambodia	Malaysia
China	Thailand	Indonesia	Mongolia
Myanmar	Korea, DR	Vietnam	Korea, Rep.
Papua New Guinea			

EUROPE AND CENTRAL ASIA (2)

Albania	Hungary	Russian Federation	Armenia
Azerbaijan	Kazakhstan	Tajikistan	Belarus
Kyrgyzstan	Turkey	Bosnia & Herzegovina	Latvia
Turkmenia	Bulgaria	Lithuania	Ukraine
Croatia	Uzbekistan	Moldova	Yugoslavia
Estonia	Poland	Georgia	Romania

LATIN AMERICA AND THE CARIBBEAN (3)

Ecuador	Paraguay	Argentina	El Salvador
Peru	Bolivia	Guatemala	Brazil
Chile	Haiti	Colombia	Honduras
Trinidad and Tobago	Costa Rica	Jamaica	Uruguay
Cuba	Mexico	Venezuela	Nicaragua
Dominican Republic	Panama		

MIDDLE EAST AND NORTH AFRICA (4)

Algeria	Jordan	Saudi Arabia	Lebanon
Syria	Egypt	Libya	Tunisia
Iran	Morocco	United Arab Emirates	Iraq
Oman	Yemen		

SOUTH ASIA (5)

Afghanistan	India	Pakistan	Bangladesh
Sri Lanka	Bhutan	Nepal	

SUB-SAHARAN AFRICA (6)

Angola	Gabon	Nigeria	Benin
Rwanda	Botswana	Ghana	Burkina Faso
Guinea	Senegal	Burundi	Guinea-Bissau
Cameroon	Kenya	Sierra Leone	Lesotho
Somalia	Central African Republic	Liberia	South Africa
Chad	Madagascar	Sudan	Malawi
Congo, Democratic Republic	Mali	Tanzania	Mauritania
Togo	Côte d'Ivoire	Mauritius	Uganda
Zambia	Mozambique	Zimbabwe	Namibia
Ethiopia	Niger		

NORTH AMERICA (7)

United States	Canada

OCEANIA (8)

Australia	New Zealand

Appendix F
Coastal States

Albania	Algeria	Angola	Argentina
Australia	Azerbaijan	Bangladesh	Belgium
Benin	Bosnia & Herzegovina	Brazil	Bulgaria
Cambodia	Cameroon	Canada	China
Chile	Colombia	Congo	Costa Rica
Cote d'Ivoire	Croatia	Cuba	Denmark
Dominican Republic	Ecuador	Egypt	El Salvador
Estonia	Finland	France	Gabon
Georgia	Germany	Ghana	Guatemala
Guinea	Guinea-Bissau	Greece	Haiti
Honduras	India	Indonesia	Iran
Italy	Jamaica	Japan	Jordan
Kazakhstan	Kenya	Kuwait	Latvia
Liberia	Libya	Lithuania	Madagascar
Malaysia	Mauritania	Mexico	Morocco
Mozambique	Myanmar	Namibia	Netherlands
New Zealand	Nicaragua	Nigeria	North Korea
Norway	Oman	Pakistan	Panama
Papua New Guinea	Peru	Philippines	Poland
Portugal	Romania	Russia	Saudi Arabia
Senegal	Sierra Leone	Slovenia	Somalia
South Africa	South Korea	Spain	Sudan
Sweden	Syria	Taiwan	Tanzania
Thailand	Togo	Trinidad/Tobago	Tunisia
Turkey	Turkmenistan	Ukraine	United Arab Emirates
United Kingdom	United States	Uruguay	Venezuela
Vietnam	Yemen	Yugoslavia	Zaire

Notes

NOTES FOR CHAPTER ONE

1. Jesse H. Ausubel, "The Liberation of the Environment," *Daedalus* 125, no. 3 (1996): 1.
2. Since 1900, the world's population has multiplied more than three times and its economy has grown twenty-fold. The consumption of fossil fuels has grown by a factor of thirty, and industrial production by a factor of fifty. Most of that growth occurred since 1950 and much of it is unsustainable. But it is also important to note that the increases in global production, consumption, and disposal have highly differential consequences, depending on the location in which they are taking place.
3. Andrew Hurrell and Benedict Kingsbury, eds., *The International Politics of the Environment* (Oxford: Oxford University Press, 1992): v.
4. The other fundamental areas of international relations theory are: 1) security or traditional international relations; and, 2) economics or international political economy.
5. Ann Florini, Julian Emmons, and Laura Strohm, *How Does Social Science Help Solve Environmental Problems* (Los Angeles: University of California, 1992): 1.
6. Florini, Emmons, and Strohm, 1.
7. Florini, Emmons, and Strohm, 2.
8. Harold Jacobson and Edith Brown Weiss, "Strengthening Compliance with International Environmental Accords: Preliminary Observations from a Collaborative Project," *Global Governance* (1995): 119.

NOTES FOR CHAPTER TWO

1. Florini, Emmons, and Strohm, 1.
2. Florini, Emmons, and Strohm, 1–2.
3. Florini, Emmons, and Strohm, 1.
4. Florini, Emmons, and Strohm, 5.
5. According to Hurrell and Kingsbury, the overall climate of international relations affects the kinds of issues that find prominence on the international agenda. For instance, international concern for the environment in the

early 1970s coincided with a period of détente between the USSR and the United States. Furthermore, with the end of the Cold War, the international community has shown increased concern for the environment. For further discussion, see Andrew Hurrell and Benedict Kingsbury, 21.

6. See Kenneth Waltz, *Theory of International Politics* (Reading, MA: Addison-Wesley, 1979).

7. Robert Keohane and Joseph Nye, "The Characteristics of Complex Interdependence," ed. Robert Keohane and Joseph Nye, Power and Interdependence (Upper Saddle River, NJ: Scott, Foreman and Co., 1977).

8. Cooperative strategies and solutions to international environmental problems, as reflected in regime theory, are central themes in major works on international environmental politics. Important texts using this approach include: 1) Gareth Porter and Janet Welsh Brown, Global Environmental Politics (Boulder, CO: Westview Press, 1991); 2) Hurrell and Kingsbury; 3) Robert Keohane and Marc Levy, *Institutions for the Earth* (Cambridge, MA: MIT Press, 1993); and, 4) Tony Brenton, The Greening of Machiavelli (London, UK: Earthscan, 1994)

9. See Susan Strange "Cave! Hic Dragones: A Critique of Regime Analysis," *International Organization*, 32, no. 2 (1982): 479–493 for a further critique of regime theory.

10. J. Samuel Barkin and George F. Shambaugh, eds., *Anarchy and the Environment: The International Relations of Common Pool Resources* (Albany: State University of New York Press, 1999), ix.

11. J. Samuel Barkin and George F. Shambaugh, ix.

12. Non-state actors include individuals, non-governmental organizations (NGOs), international non-governmental organizations (INGOs), "epistemic communities," multinational corporations (MNCs) and other for-profit organizations.

13. See Barbara J. Bramble and Gareth Porter, "Non-Governmental Organizations and the Making of U.S. International Environmental Policy," eds. Andrew Hurrell and Benedict Kingsbury, 313–354 for one such example of this literature.

14. See Michael Doyle, "Liberalism and World Politics," APSR, 88, no. 4 (1986): 1151–1169; David Lake, "Powerful Pacifists: Democratic States and War," APSR, 86, no. 1 (1992): 24–37; and, Carol R. Ember, Melvin Ember and Bruce Russett, "Peace Between Participatory Polities," *World Politics*, 44 (1992): 573–99 for further discussion of the democratic influence.

15. Karen Liftin "Ecoregimes: Playing Tug of War with the Nation-State," eds. Ronnie Lipschutz and Ken Conca, *The State and Social Power in Global Environmental Politics* (New York: Columbia University Press, 1993), 95.

16. See Hans Morgenthau, "Six Principles of Political Realism," eds. Phil Williams, Donald M. Goldstein and Jay M. Shafritz, *Classical Readings of International Relations* (Florence, KY: Wadsworth 1994), for a discussion of this theoretical approach.

17. Lynton Caldwell, "The Stockholm Conference and Its Legacy, 1972–1992," *International Environmental Policy* (Durham, N.C.: Duke University Press, 1984), 83.

18. See Joseph Grieco, "Anarchy and the Limits of Cooperation," *International Organization*, 42, no. 3 (1988); Duncan Snidal, "Relative Gains and the Pattern of International Cooperation," APSR, 85, no. 3 (1991): 701–26; and, Robert Powell "Absolute and Relative Gains in International Relations Theory," APSR, 85, no. 4 (1991): 1303–1320.

19. Rodney White, *North, South, and the Environmental Crisis* (Toronto: University of Toronto Press, 1993), 161.

20. Thomas Homer-Dixon, "Environmental Scarcities and Violent Conflict," *International Security*, 19:1 (1994): 45.

21. Thomas Homer-Dixon, "Environmental Scarcities and Violent Conflict," 44.

22. World Commission on Environment and Development, *Our Common Future* (Oxford: Oxford University Press, 1987), 292.

23. Arthur Westing, ed., Global Resources and International Conflict: *Environmental Factors in Strategic Policy and Action* (Oxford: Oxford University Press, 1987).

24. Thomas Homer-Dixon, "No. 300: Environmental Scarcity and Global Security," Foreign Policy Association (1987), 7.

25. Hugh Dyer, "EcoCultures: Global Culture in the Age of Ecology," *Millenium: Journal of International Studies*, 22, no. 3 (1993): 483–504.

26. Nancy Lee Peluso, "Coercing Conservation," eds. Lipschutz, Ronnie and Ken Conca, 49.

27. Lamont Hempel, *Environmental Governance: The Global Challenge* (Washington, D.C.: Island Press, 1996), 151.

28. Nils Petter Gleditsch and Bjorn Otto Sverdrup, *Democracy and the Environment* (Oslo: International Peace Research Institute, 1995), 1.

29. Environmental externalities are defined as the unintended by-products of production or consumption.

30. See David Pearce, Edward Barbier, and Anil Markandya, Sustainable Development: Economics and the Environment in the Third World (London: Edward Elgar, 1990).

31. The UN system of national accounts, which places primary emphasis on Gross Domestic Product as a measure of economic performance, has been used by states and international monetary organizations (i.e., World Bank) since its inception in 1968.

32. See J.R. Blodgett, Jr., *Environmental Policy and the Economy: Conflicts and Concordances [CRS Report 95–147 ENR]*, US Library of Congress: Congressional Research Service, January 10, 1995; and, ESRC Global Environmental Change Programme, Making of Environmental Decisions: Cost-Benefit Analysis, Contingent Valuation and Alternatives (Center for the Study of Environmental Change and Green Practitioner's Seminar, 1997).

33. Peter J. Katzenstein, ed., *The Culture of National Security: Norms and Identity in World Politics* (N.Y.: Columbia University Press, 1996).

34. Eric Eckholm, *Down to Earth: Environment and Human Needs* (N.Y.: W.W. Norton and Company, 1982), 5.

35. Heather Rae and Chris Reus-Smit, eds., *The United Nations: Between Sovereignty and Global Governance?* (Melbourne: La Trobe University, 1995), 6.

36. The distribution of relative capabilities across states in the international system results in power configurations known as unipolarity, bipolarity or multipolarity. Each power configuration has distinct characteristics that in turn influence state behavior, especially in regard to the prospects for cooperation or conflict.

37. States will engage in cooperative activities when it promotes their national interests, enhances their power position, or ensures survival in the international system.

38. Interdependence is defined as "changes or events in any single part of a system will produce some reaction or have some significant consequence in other parts of the system." See Bruce Russett and Harvey Starr, *World Politics: Menu for Choice* (N.Y.: W.H. Freeman and Company, 1996), 76.

39. Lamont Hempel, 155.

40. Lamont Hempel, 155.

41. See Oran R. Young, "The Politics of International Regime Formation: Managing Natural Resources and the Environment," International Organization, 43 (1989): 349–375; and, Oran R. Young, International *Governance: Protecting the Environment in a Stateless Society* (Ithaca: Cornell University Press, 1994).

42. See Oran R. Young, *International Governance: Protecting the Environment in a Stateless Society,* 27–28 for a further description of this approach.

43. Stephen D. Krasner, "Structural Causes and Regime Consequences: Regimes as Intervening Variables," ed. Stephen D. Krasner, *International Regimes* (Ithaca: Cornell University Press, 1983), 2.

44. See Robert Keohane, "A Functional Theory of Regimes," eds. Art and Jervis, *International Politics: Enduring Concepts and Contemporary Issues,* (N.Y.: Harper Collins Publishers, 1992), 95–101 and Robert Keohane, "The Demand for International Regimes," ed. Stephen Krasner, *International Regimes,* 14–171.

45. Karen Liftin, "Eco-regimes: Playing Tug of War with the Nation-State," 10.

46. Heather Rae and Chris Reus-Smit, 5–6.

47. See Wesley T. Wooley, *Alternatives to Anarchy: American Supranationalism Since World War II,* (Bloomington: Indiana University Press, 1988); and, Elinor Ostrom, *Governing the Commons: The Evolution of Institutions for Collective Action,* (N.Y.: Cambridge University Press, 1990).

48. Paul Wapner, "Reorienting State Sovereignty: Rights and Responsibilities in the Environmental Age," ed. Karen Liftin, *The Greening of Sovereignty in World Politics* (Cambridge: MIT Press, 1998), 275–297.

49. Paul Wapner, 288.

50. See Hedley Bull, *The Anarchical Society: A Study of Order in World Politics,* (London: Macmillan, 1977) for a discussion of problems associated with transcending the state system.

51. Andrew Hurrell and Benedict Kingsbury, 7.

52. Andrew Hurrell and Benedict Kingsbury, 8.

53. Andrew Hurrell and Benedict Kingsbury, 37.

54. The UN International Court of Justice, for example, does make judgments on the activities of states, though the UN has thus far never enforced these decisions.

55. Harold K. Jacobson and Judith Brown Weiss, "Strengthening Compliance with International Environmental Accords: Preliminary Observations from a Collaborative Project," 120.
56. Lamont Hempel, 123–124. Also see Patricia Birnie, "International Environmental Law: Its Adequacy for Present and Future Needs," ed. Andrew Hurrell and Benedict Kingsbury, 51–84; and Lawrence Susskind and Connie Ozawa, "Negotiating More Effective International Environmental Agreements," Andrew Hurrell and Benedict Kingsbury, 142–165 for further discussion.
57. Lamont Hempel, 21.
58. Lamont Hempel, 149–165.
59. Here I am referring to the realist assumption of the state as a rational and unitary actor.
60. See Michael Doyle, "Liberalism and World Politics."
61. Nils Petter Gleditsch and Bjorn Otto Sverdrup, 1.
62. Nils Petter Gleditsch and Bjorn Otto Sverdrup, 2.
63. See William M. Lafferty, Natur & Miljo (1993): 23–24; Thomas Wyller, *"The Ecological Crisis: A Problem of Democratic Political Power,"* Paper presented at the 16th World Congress of Political Science, Berlin, 21–25 August, 1994; William Ophuls, *Ecology and the Politics of Scarcity: Prologue to a Political Theory of the Steady State,* (San Francisco, CA.: Freeman, 1977); and, John Passmore, *Man's Responsibility for Nature,* (London: Duckworth, 1974).
64. Nils Petter Gleditsch and Bjorn Otto Sverdrup, 5–6.
65. Harold Jacobson and Edith Brown Weiss, "Strengthening Compliance with International Environmental Accords: Preliminary Observations from a Collaborative Project," 119.
66. Harold Jacobson and Edith Brown Weiss, "Strengthening Compliance with International Environmental Agreements," *Woodrow Wilson Environmental Change and Security Project Report,* Issue 3, Spring 1997, 1157.
67. Issue areas include: climate change, ozone depletion, deforestation, biodiversity, and drinking water.
68. Nils Petter Gleditsch and Bjorn Otto Sverdrup, 20.
69. Jacqueline Vaughn Switzer with Gary Bryner, *Environmental Politics: Domestic and Global Dimensions,* 2nd Edition, (N.Y.: St. Martin's Press, 1998), 36.
70. Bruce Russett and Harvey Starr, 67.
71. Bruce Russett and Harvey Starr, 68.
72. Switzer and Bryner, 36.
73. Switzer and Bryner, 36.
74. Bruce Russett and Harvey Starr, 68.
75. According to *The Yearbook of International Organizations (1997),* in 1956 there were 985 active NGOs. Currently, there are over 20,000. See Lester Brown, Michael Renner, and Brian Halweil, Vital Signs, (N.Y.: Worldwatch Institute, 1999), 188; and, Lester M. Salamon and Helmut K. Anheier, *The Emerging Sector Revisited: A Summary of Initial Estimates,* (Baltimore: John Hopkins, 1998).

76. Liftin notes NGOs were key actors in the negotiation, implementation, and monitoring of virtually all existing international environmental agreements. See Karen Liftin, "Eco-regimes: Playing Tug of War with the Nation-State," 95.
77. Lamont Hempel, 5.
78. David Malin Roodman, "Building a Sustainable Society," State of the World 1999 (N.Y.: Worldwatch Institute, 1999), 183.
79. See Andrew Hurrell and Benedict Kingsbury, 20 for further discussion.
80. This approach challenges assumptions that claim the international system is transparent enough for actors to clearly identify their own interests as well as interpret the signals and behavior of other actors.
81. Emanuel Alder and Peter Haas, "Conclusion: Epistemic Communities, World Order and the Creation of a Reflective Research Program," *International Organization,* 46, no. 1, (1992): 367–390.
82. Nancy Lee Peluso, "Coercing Conservation: The Politics of State Resource Control," eds. Ronnie D. Lipschutz and Ken Conca, 49.
83. Alexander Wendt, "Anarchy Is What States Make of It," *International Organization,* 46, no. 2, (1992): 391–425.
84. Karen T. Liftin, *The Greening of Sovereignty in World Politics,* 4.
85. According to Lipschutz and Conca, institutions (whether political, social or economic) include: 1) the political ordering of states, 2) the activities of international organization and transnational movements; and, 3) the ordinary and mundane practices of people as they go about their daily routines. See Ronnie D. Lipschutz and Ken Conca, eds., 119 for further discussion.
86. Ann Hawkins, "Contested Ground: International Environmentalism and Global Climate Change," eds. Ronnie D. Lipschutz and Ken Conca, 227.
87. See Anne Hawkins, 221–245 for further discussion of these models.
88. This approach does not necessarily argue that the state is being replaced by new forms of global governance, only that these governing mechanisms may be modifying state behavior in the environmental realm.

NOTE FOR CHAPTER THREE

1. Jesse Ausubel, "The Liberation of the Environment," *Daedalus,* 125, no. 3 (1996): 1–2.
2. Jesse Ausubel, 1–2.
3. Jesse Ausubel, 1–2.
4. Jesse Ausubel, 1–2.
5. Two important texts produced during this period were John Evelyn's *Fumifuguim,* often considered the first book on air pollution, and Grotius Mare Liberum's *Freedom of the Sea,* the first text on international law.
6. Tony Brenton, 16.
7. This whaling convention led to the establishment of the International Whaling Commission in 1946.
8. The *International Convention for the Regulation of Whaling* (1946) is often cited as the most notable example of an international environmental treaty that despite overwhelming international concern, lacked sufficient international support to be an effective instrument.

9. According to this view, one did economically well by doing ecologically bad.
10. This treaty dealt with pollution associated with discharge of oil from tankers into oceans.
11. Tony Brenton, 18.
12. Tony Brenton, xiii.
13. Parties to these regional agreement negotiated a second convention in 1972 (Oslo Convention of 1972), whereby they agreed to limit and regulate the dumping of wastes into seas and oceans.
14. (GAR 1803[xvii])
15. The experts attending this conference agreed that environmental degradation had reached a critical level. These findings paved the way for the United Nations Conference on the Human Environment to be held in Stockholm in 1972.
16. U.N. General Assembly Resolution 2398.
17. Tony Brenton, 34.
18. See Ronald Inglehart, *The Silent Revolution: Changing Values and Political Styles Among Western Publics* (Princeton: Princeton University Press, 1977).
19. Jacqueline Vaughn Switzer with Gary Bryner, 36.
20. One such example of public activity was Earth Day April 22, 1970 in which 20 million people in the United States participated.
21. The Sprout's work is also important because their notions of interdependence foreshadow the work of Keohane and Nye in 1989.
22. For a more detailed discussion of the Club of Rome's findings see Donella H. Meadows, Dennis L. Meadows, Jorgen Randers, and William W. Behrens III, *The Limits to Growth: A Report for the Club of Rome's Project on the Predicament of Mankind* (New York: Universe Books, 1972).
23. Richard Falk, *Democratizing, Internationalizing and Globalizing: A Collage of Blurred Images*, Conference Paper, March 24–27, 1992, "Changing World Order and the United Nations System," Yokohmam, Japan, p. 10.
24. Tony Brenton, 5.
25. See the following books for a discussion of conflicting opinions regarding "limits to growth": Mihajlo Mesarovic and Eduard Pestel, Mankind at the Turning Point (N.Y.: Dutton, 1974); Amilcar Herrera, et. al., Catastrophe or New Society (International Development Research Centre, 1976); Herman Kahn, William Brown, and Leon Martel, The Next 200 Years (N.Y.: William Morrow, 1976); Julian Simon, The Ultimate Resource (N.J.: Princeton University Press, (1981); Julian Simon and Herman Kahn, *The Resourceful Earth* (Oxford: Basil Blackwell, 1984); and, Max Singer, *Passage to a Human World* (Indianapolis, Indiana, Hudson Institute, 1987).
26. Tony Brenton, 45.
27. Tony Brenton, 47.
28. United Nations agencies with environmental responsibilities established prior to Stockholm include the IAEA for atomic energy; FAO for agriculture and forests; UNESCO for science, and WHO for environmental health.

Additionally, the World Bank appointed its first environmental advisor in 1970 and announced at Stockholm that environmental assessment would be integral part of project preparation.

29. Tony Brenton, 49.
30. UNEP is located in Kenya, Africa.
31. Erik Eckholm, 5.
32. See Paragraph B, Stockholm Recommendation 103; Resolution 3002 [xxvii] of General Assembly 15 December 1972; or Stockholm Recommendation 107 or 109 for further discussion of rights and responsibilities of states in regard to international environmental assistance.
33. Lynton Caldwell, 66.
34. Lynton Caldwell, 83.
35. CITES was particularly important because it set a precedent which demonstrated the effectiveness of using national self-interest and trade measures to promote environmental ends.
36. Ten years after Stockholm, three of these treaties were at least technically in effect. MARPOL came into force 10/2/83 one year after it received the required number of ratifications.
37. Tony Brenton, 54.
38. Tony Brenton, 54.
39. UNCTAD has traditionally been one forum through which the developing countries have attempted to change not only the terms of international trade, but advance their proposed model of economic development.
40. Tony Brenton, 69.
41. Tony Brenton, 67.
42. Tony Brenton, 69.
43. Emergence of environmental policy in the North was a bottom-up process whereby popular concern rapidly communicated itself to democratically elected governments and protection of environment became an agreed upon objective for public policy.
44. Marine pollution treaties accounted for slightly less than half of all the treaties negotiated both over the whole period and in the two decades following Stockholm.
45. The developed countries dominated the agenda of many of these negotiations.
46. The materials covered by this treaty were extended from oil to all substances.
47. In fact, in 1978 there still were not enough signatures for the treaty to be entered into force.
48. James Lee Ray, Global Politics, 7th Edition (Boston: Houghton Mifflin Company, 1998), 282.
49. These treaties include the World Heritage Convention, the London Dumping Convention, CITES, and MARPOL to name only a few.
50. Including UNCLOS, NIEO, and UNCOD.
51. World Resources Institute, *World Resources* 1994–1995 (NY: Oxford University Press, 1994), 224.
52. Environmental and climatic disasters of this era include: chemical plant explosion in Bhopal India (1984); drought in Ethiopia (1984); floods in

Bangladesh in (1984); industrial explosions in Cubatao, Brazil and Mexico City (1984); famine in Sub-Sahara (1985); a cyclone in Bangladesh (1985); an earthquake in Mexico (1985); discovery of ozone hole (1985); Chernobyl accident (1986); major fire at Swiss chemical factory which extensively polluted the Rhine (1986); renewed famine in Ethiopia and worst hurricane for a century in UK (1987); 1988 global climate change with 1983, 1987 and 1981, 1988 hottest years since record began.

53. The *World Charter for Nature* came about as a result of the developing countries' initiative. It sets out 24 mandatory conservation duties for nations and individuals.

54. Sustainable development has been defined as "the process of change in which the exploitation of resources, the direction of investments, the orientation of technological development, and institutional changes are made consistent with future as well as present needs." See World Commission on Environment and Development, 9. Tony Brenton provides another definition: "development which meets the needs of the present without compromising the ability of future generations to meet their own needs." Tony Brenton, 129.

55. This session paralleled the evaluation of the Action Plan undertaken by the UN that same year.

56. Antarctica is administered through regular meetings of thirty-eight states that have laid claims to the continent.

57. These material interests include: biodiversity, climate change and imports of tropical wood.

58. It appears likely that the high-level of western government interest in this issue was a response to popular environmentalism.

59. Tony Brenton, 5.

60. Tony Brenton, 214.

61. Tony Brenton, xv.

62. The US demanded that the need to observe and enforce intellectual demands be included in the language in Agenda 21.

63. Tony Brenton, 221.

64. Tony Brenton, 221.

65. Tony Brenton, 221.

66. Tony Brenton, 231.

67. The negotiation process and recommendations of Stockholm were rarely quoted at the Rio conference or in the resulting texts.

68. If participants had understood the implications of the North-South divide, they might have been able to avoid many of the same debates that emerged at Rio.

69. Tony Brenton, 234.

70. "GEO: Global Environmental Outlook 3: Multilateral environmental arrangements," *United Nations Environmental Programme*, 2004, 61. <http://www.unep.org/GEO/geo3/English/061.htm>

71. "GEO: Global Environmental Outlook 3: Multilateral environmental arrangements," 61.

72. "GEO: Global Environmental Outlook 3: The Convention on Biological Diversity," *United Nations Environmental Programme*, 2004, 62. <http://www.unep.org/GEO/geo3/English/062.htm>

73. "GEO: Global Environmental Outlook 3: The Convention on Biological Diversity," 62.

74. "GEO: Global Environmental Outlook 3: The Convention to Combat Desertification," *United Nations Environmental Programme*, 2004, 63. <http://www.unep.org/GEO/geo3/English/063.htm>

75. "GEO: *Global Environmental Outlook 3: The Convention to Combat Desertification,*" 63.

76. *Radford University, Environmental History Timeline.* <http://www.radford.edu/~wkovarik/hist1/12oughties.html>

77. "The Global Phase-out of Leaded Gasoline: A Successful Initiative," *Earth Summit Watch*. 1999. <http://www.earthsummitwatch.org/gasoline.html>

78. Radford University, Environmental History Timeline.

79. Radford University, Environmental History Timeline.

80. Radford University, Environmental History Timeline.

81. Radford University, Environmental History Timeline.

82. "GEO: Global Environmental Outlook 3: Rio +5," *United Nations Environmental Programme*, 2004, 65. <http://www.unep.org/GEO/geo3/English/065.htm>

83. "RESOLUTION ADOPTED BY THE GENERAL ASSEMBLY [without reference to a Main Committee (A/S-19/29)]" *United Nations General Assembly*, September 19, 1997 <http://www.un.org/documents/ga/res/spec/aress19-2.htm>

84. "RESOLUTION ADOPTED BY THE GENERAL ASSEMBLY [without reference to a Main Committee (A/S-19/29)]"

85. Radford University, Environmental History Timeline.

86. "GEO: Global Environmental Outlook 3: Globalization," *United Nations Environmental Programme*, 2004, 76. <http://www.unep.org/GEO/geo3/English/076.htm>

87. "GEO: Global Environmental Outlook 3: Globalization"

88. "GEO: Global Environmental Outlook 3: Globalization"

89. "Malmo Ministerial Declaration," *United Nations Environmental Programme*, <http://www.unep.org/malmo/malmo_ministerial.htm>

90. GEO: Global Environmental Outlook 3: The Millennium Summit," *United Nations Environmental Programme*, 2004, 72. <http://www.unep.org/GEO/geo3/English/072.htm>

91. Radford University, Environmental History Timeline.

92. The Wilderness Society of the United States complained that the Bush plan was half century out of date. See: Radford University, Environmental History Timeline.

93. Radford University, Environmental History Timeline.

94. GEO: Global Environmental Outlook 3: Climate and energy consumption," *United Nations Environmental Programme*, 2004, 73. <http://www.unep.org/GEO/geo3/English/073.htm>

95. "GEO: *Global Environmental Outlook 3: Climate and energy consumption,*"

96. Radford University, Environmental History Timeline.

97. Radford University, Environmental History Timeline.

98. Radford University, Environmental History Timeline.

99. Radford University, Environmental History Timeline.
100. Radford University, Environmental History Timeline.
101. *"Johannesburg Summit* 2002," United Nations, March 2003, <http://www.johannesburgsummit.org/>
102. Radford University, Environmental History Timeline.
103. Radford University, Environmental History Timeline.
104. Radford University, Environmental History Timeline.
105. Tony Brenton, 25.
106. Tony Brenton, 257.
107. Tony Brenton, 85.
108. Tony Brenton, 241.
109. See Ronald Inglehart, *The Silent Revolution: Changing Values and Political Styles Among Western Publics* (Princeton: Princeton University Press, 1977).
110. Tony Brenton, 263.
111. Tony Brenton, 85.
112. Tony Brenton, 264.
113. Tony Brenton, 264.
114. Lynton Caldwell, 83.

NOTES FOR CHAPTER FOUR

1. Ann Florini, Julian Emmons and Laura Strohm, 1.
2. Ann Florini, Julian Emmons and Laura Strohm, 1.
3. Ann Florini, Julian Emmons and Laura Strohm, 2.
4. Samuel J.Barkin and George E. Shambaugh, ix.
5. Samuel J.Barkin and George E. Shambaugh, ix.
6. Harold Jacobson and Edith Brown Weiss, "Strengthening Compliance with International Environmental Accords: Preliminary Observations from a Collaborative Project," 119.
7. Heather Rae and Chris Reus-Smit, eds., 2.
8. The population of treaties was compiled from the *United Nations Register of International Treaties and Other Agreements in the Field of the Environment* (2000).
9. For the purposes of this study, "regional" is defined as a segment of the world bound together by a common set of geographic, social, cultural, economic and political ties.
10. It should be noted that the population of treaties examined in this study includes the original treaties and amendments and protocols to the original treaties. Amendments and protocols are included in this study because they emerge directly from the original treaties, cover specific issues contained within those treaties, and offer more stringent regulations for dealing with those specific issues. See Appendix I for a listing of international environmental treaties included in this study.
11. Sovereignty in this context refers to the year a state entered the international system.
12. States with a population of fewer than one million, and international trustees or safe zones are not included in this study.

13. See Appendix 2 for a list of states included in this study as well as years of their inclusion.
14. Peter Harris-Jones, Abraham Rotstein and Peter Timmerman, "Nature's Veto: UNCED and the Debate over the Earth," Working Group of Science for Peace (Toronto: University of Toronto, 1992).
15. World Resources Institute, World Resources 1994–1995 (NY: Oxford University Press, 1994), 224.
16. Articles 10 and 18 of the Vienna Convention on the Law of Treaties (1969).
17. Articles 2(1)(b), 14(1) and 16, Vienna Convention on the Law of Treaties (1969).
18. Articles 2(1)(b), 14(1) and 16, Vienna Convention on the Law of Treaties (1969).
19. Articles 2(1)(b) and 14(2), Vienna Convention on the Law of Treaties (1969).
20. Articles 2(1)(b) and 15, Vienna Convention on the Law of Treaties (1969).
21. Constance Mungall and Degby J. Mclaren, *The Challenge of Global Climate Change: Planet Under Stress* (Toronto: Oxford University Press, 1991), 288.
22. M.W. Holdgate, A *Perspective of Environmental Pollution* (Cambridge: Cambridge University Press, 1979), 7.
23. Based on the definitions provided above, the treaty texts for the thirty-eight international environmental treaties were examined in order to determine whether each of the international environmental treaties included in this study would be coded as essentially resource management or pollution control oriented. The treaty texts were acquired from the *United Nations Register of International Treaties and Other Agreement in the Field of the Environment (2002)*. Pollution control treaties were coded as zero (0), while resource management treaties were coded as one (1).
24. Mathias Finger, "The Military, the Nation-State and the Environment," The Ecologist, 21:5 (1991): 224.
25. The texts were obtained from the *United Nations Register of International Treaties and Other Agreement in the Field of the Environment* (2000). These five treaties were coded as one (1), while the remaining international environmental treaties (that did not require a state to alter its military behavior) were coded as zero.
26. Information regarding state possession of weapons of mass destruction and military capabilities for the purpose of environmental modification were gathered from the following sources: Monterey Institute of International Studies, "Center for Nonproliferation Studies" <http://cns.miis.edu/>; Carnegie Endowment for International Peace, "Nuclear Nonproliferation Project" <http://www.ceip.org/files/nonprolif/default.asp>; the US Arms Control and Disarmament Agency, <http://dosfan.lib.uic.edu/acda/>; the US Department of Defense <http://www.defenselink.mil/>; the Central Intelligence Agency <http://www.cia.gov/>; and, the International Institute for Strategic Studies <http://www.iiss.org/>. Using information gathered from these various sources; states without nuclear and/or biological weapons or capabilities, as well as the military capabilities to modify the

environment were coded as zero (0). States with undeclared or suspected nuclear or biological weapons programs, as well as military capabilities to modify the environment were coded as one (1). While, declared nuclear and biological weapon states, Soviet successor states with nuclear or biological weapons on their territory, and states with the technical capacity to operate nuclear weapons or possess stocks of weapon-usable nuclear material were coded as two (2).

27. Lawrence Susskind and Connie Ozawa, "Negotiating More Effective International Environmental Agreements," ed. Andrew Hurrell and Benedict Kingsbury, 143.

28. When the primary responsibility of paying for the costs of adoption and implementation of a specific international environmental treaty was assigned to an individual or specified collection of states, the treaty was coded as zero (0). When the responsibility for paying for the costs of the treaty was equitably distributed among the parties of the treaty, the treaty was coded as one (1).

29. Technological transfers, in this context, refer to the knowledge, skills, methods, designs, specialized equipment, etc. necessary for the long-term success of implementation.

30. In the event that technological transfers were not mentioned in the treaty text, those international environmental treaties were coded as zero (0). Where technological transfers were mentioned, those treaties were coded as one (1).

31. In the event that the treaty text made no mention of creating or establishing monitoring mechanisms, the international environmental treaty was coded as zero (0). When the creation or establishment of a monitoring mechanism was explicitly stated in the treaty text, the treaty was coded as one (1).

32. A.F.K. Organski, Bruce Bueno de Mesquita, and Alan Lamborn "The Effective Population in International Politics," ed. A. E. Keir Nash, Governance and Population: The Governmental Implications of Population Change (Washington, D.C.: Government Printing Office, 1972), 237–249.

33. A.F.K. Organski, and Jacek Kugler, The War Ledger (Chicago: Chicago University Press, 1980), 30.

34. A.F.K. Organski, and Jacek Kugler, 30–38.

35. A.F.K. Organski, and Jacek Kugler, 34.

36. A.F.K. Organski, and Jacek Kugler, 38.

37. The GNP for the states included in this study was collected for the years 1972–2002 using the following sources: the Consortium for International Earth Science Information Network (2002) *ENTRI Database; the World Bank's World Development Indicators, 2002;* and, the World Resource Institute.

38. "Great powers" are defined as large states that possess especially great military and economic strength, hence influence. According to Joshua Goldstein there are seven great powers in the international system: United States, Japan, Germany, France, Britain, Russia and China. See Joshua Goldstein, *International Relations* (New York: Longman, 1999), 83.

39. L.D. Guruswamy, "Global Warming: Integrating the United States and International Law," Arizona Law Review, 32 (1990), 221–278.

40. The following texts proved invaluable to this process: 1) "Background to the United Nations Conference on Environment and Development," *The Globe*, 7 (1992); 2) Tony Brent, *The Greening of Machiavelli* (Washington, D.D.: The Brookings Institute, 1994); 3) Lester R. Brown, et. al., *Worldwatch Institute: State of the World 1990* (NY: WW Norton, 1990); 4) Lester R. Brown, et. al., *Worldwatch Institute: State of the World 1991* (NY: WW Norton, 1991); 5) Lynton Caldwell, *International Environmental Policy* (Chapel Hill, N.C.: Duke University Press, 1997); 6) Eric Eckholm, *Down to Earth—Environment and Human Needs* (New Delhi: Affiliated East-West Press Pvt Ltd, 1982); 7) John M. Fitzgerald, "The Biological Diversity Treaty of the United Nations Conference on Environment and Development," *Endangered Species Update*, 9, no. 9 and 10 (1992); 8) Lamont C. Hempel, *Environmental Governance: The Global Challenge* (Island Press, 1996); 9) Martin W. Holdgate, Mohammed Kassas, and Gilbert F. White, eds., *The World Environment* 1972–1982 (Dublin: Tycooly International Publishing Limited, 1982); 10) Clyde Sanger, *Ordering the Oceans: The Making of the Law of the Sea* (London: Zed Books, 1986); 11) Daniel Sitarz, Agenda 21 (Boulder, Colorado: Earthpress, 1993); 12) Mostafa K. Tolba, ed., *Evolving Environmental Perceptions: From Stockholm to Nairobi* (London: Butterworths, 1988); 13) Mostafa K. Tolba, et. al., *The World Environment* 1972–1992: *Two Decades of Challenge* (London: Chapman and Hall, 1992); 14) Mostafa K. Tolba and Iwona Rummel-Bulska, *Global Environmental Diplomacy: Negotiating Environmental Agreements for the World 1973–1992* (Cambridge: MIT Press, 1998); 15) Rodney White, *North, South, and the Environmental Crisis* (Toronto: Toronto University Press, 1993); and, 16) World Commission on Environment and Development, *Our Common Future* (Oxford: Oxford University Press, 1987). International environmental treaties in which "great powers" did not provide active leadership during the negotiation process were coded as zero (0). Where "great powers" provided a leadership role, those treaties were coded one (1).

41. The World Bank developed this classification scheme over thirty years ago for the purpose of classifying states into three income groups (low, middle, and high) using a comparative ranking of states. The thresholds established by the World Bank are updated yearly by measures of international inflation with a state's GNP.

42. States with low-income economies were coded as zero (0); middle-income economies were coded as one (1); and, high-income economies were coded as two (2).

43. See Appendix III.

44. See Michael Doyle, "On the Democratic Peace."

45. Nils Petter Gleditsch and Bjorn Otto Sverdrup, *Democracy and the Environment*. 2.

46. Levels of freedom were established by Freedom House (2000) *Table of Independent Countries Comparative Measures of Freedom*. Freedom House is an annual cross-national comparative survey that was first compiled for 1972–1973. Three categories or "levels" of freedom were derived from

measures of political rights and civil liberties. Countries whose combined averages for political rights and civil liberties that fall between 1.0 and 2.5 are labeled "free," between 3.0 and 5.5 are labeled "partly free," and between 5.5 and 7.0 are labeled "not free."

47. States identified as "not-free" were coded zero (0). States identified as "partly-free" were coded one (1). While states identified as "free" were coded two (2).

48. Volker Von Prittwitz "Several Approaches to the Analysis of International Environmental Policy," in Nordal Akerman, ed., *Maintaining A Satisfactory Environment* (Boulder, Colorado: Westview Press, 1990), 7.

49. Detlef Sprinz and Tapani Vaahtoranta, "The Interest-Based Explanation for International Air Pollution Control: Determinants of Support for the Protection of the Ozone Layer and the Abatement of Acid Rain in Europe," ed. Arild Underdal, *The International Politics of Environmental Management, Dordrecht: Kluwer Academic Publishers*, 1993), 7.

50. Robert Repetto and Jonathan Lash, "Planetary Roulette: Gambling With Climate," ed. James M. Lindsay, *Perspectives: Global Issues* (Boulder: Coursewise Publishing, Inc., 1997), 45.

51. Robert Keohane and Joseph Nye, 13.

52. United Nations Environmental Programme, "Overview of Regional Status and Trends," Global Environment Outlook–1, 1997 <http://grid2.cr.usgs.gov/geo1/exsumm/ex3.htm>.

53. East Asia/Pacific was coded as (1); Europe and Central Asia were coded as (2); Latin America and the Caribbean were coded as (3); the Middle East and North Africa were coded as (4); South Asia was coded as (5); Sub-Sahara Africa was coded as (6); North America was coded as (7); and Oceania was coded as (8). See Appendix V for the classification of states into regions. 1 Non-vulnerable was coded as zero (0), less vulnerable was coded as one (1), and vulnerable was coded as two (2).

54. Three levels of vulnerability were established: non-vulnerable was coded as zero (0);

55. See Appendix VI for the classification of coastal and non-coastal states.

56. Each treaty and set of states eligible for participation in that treaty were examined in their entirety before moving to the next treaty.

57. In this case, zero (0) would represent the failure of a state to become a party to an international environmental treaty in a given year, where as a one (1) would indicate that a state did become a party to such a treaty in a particular year.

NOTES FOR CHAPTER FIVE

1. As mentioned elsewhere in this text, free-riding on international agreements is relatively easy and highly likely. It is through free-riding that states reap rewards without paying the costs.

2. The seven "great powers" are: the United States, Japan, Germany, France, Britain, Russia and China.

3. According to lesser-developed or developing states, the cause of their environmental problems was poverty. On the other hand, the developed states

      believed that developmental policies should be significantly altered in order to prevent further environmental decline.

4. The logit coefficient is 0.251, statistically significant at the .01 level of confidence.

5. Levels of freedom were established by Freedom House, *Table of Independent Countries Comparative Measures of Freedom* (2000). Freedom House is an annual cross-national comparative survey that was first compiled for 1972–1973. Three categories or "levels" of freedom were derived from measures of political rights and civil liberties. Countries whose combined averages for political rights and civil liberties that fall between 1.0 and 2.5 are labeled "free," between 3.0 and 5.5 are labeled "partly free," and between 5.5 and 7.0 are labeled "not free."

6. Detlef Sprinz and Tapani Vaahtoranta, 7; Volker Von Prittwitz, 7; Robert Repetto and Jonathan Lash, 45; and Robert Keohane and Joseph Nye, 13.

NOTES FOR CHAPTER SIX

1. For this variable there was a positive logit coefficient (0.604).

2. This convention is also known as the Convention on Biological Weapons (CBW).

3. As Joshua Goldstein notes: "Theoretically, a single weapon could spark an epidemic in an entire population." Joshua Goldstein, 272.

4. For instance, the Japanese used biological weapons on Chinese villages in WW II.

5. The potential lethality of biological weapons "strikes many leaders as a Pandora's Box that could let loose uncontrollable forces if opened." Joshua Goldstein, 272.

6. Consortium for International Earth Science Information Networks, Entri Database.

7. Harold K. Jacobson and Edith Brown Weiss, "Strengthening Compliance with International Environmental Agreements," 23–24; and, L.D. Guruswamy, 221–227.

8. Andrew Hurrell and Benedict Kingsbury, 21.

9. In the case of the Vietnam Conflict, environmental disruption was accomplished by repeated, widespread applications of herbicides, massive bombing, atmospheric manipulations, and, to a lesser extent the use of large tractors and fire.

10. An environmental modification technique is defined by the treaty as any technique for changing—through the deliberate manipulation of natural processes—the dynamics, composition, or structure of the earth (including its biota, lithosphere, hydrosphere, and atmosphere) or of outer space.

11. Arthur H. Westing, *Environmental Warfare: Manipulating the Environment for Hostile Purposes*, Environmental Change and Security Project Report Spring: ECSP Report 3 (1997).

12. Arthur H. Westing, *Environmental Warfare: Manipulating the Environment for Hostile Purposes*.

13. The more veto points that must be overcome, the less chance there is of arriving at a meaningful agreement.

14. Countries more hostile to nuclear power preferred working through the European Community, where they had a large voice, while major nuclear states preferred to work within the context of the IAEA where they had dominant influence.

15. Karen Liftin, 101.

16. In March 1967, the oil tanker Torrey Canyon ran aground off the coast of Great Britain spilling 100,000 tons of crude oil in the sea. In 1969 an oil well exploded in California's Santa Barbara Channel. Finally there was the Amoco Cadiz oil spill in 1978.

17. Of the estimated $600 billion per year needed to carry out the global environmental actions that were endorsed at Rio, the parties pledged less than $5 billion. By comparison, UN members were collectively spending an average of that amount every 44 hours on national military preparedness. Lamont C. Hempel, 35.

18. Lamont C. Hempel, 174–175.

NOTES FOR CHAPTER SEVEN

1. These channels include freedom of speech, freedom of association, and freedom of the press.

2. One only has to look at the former Soviet Union and Eastern Europe for plenty of examples.

3. States are still in fierce competition with each other in the modern international system, although this competition is now largely based on economics as opposed to military forces.

4. As already mentioned, free-riding states can then devote their resources to increasing their economic or military strength at the expense of the environment and collective efforts of states to reduce degradation. While these states increase their security, those efforts are often interpreted as potential threats by states involved in the collective undertaking.

5. Richard H. Stanley, "The United States as a World Leader," 37th Strategy for Peace Conference, October 24, 1996. <http://reports.stanleyfoundation.org/SPC96A.pdf>

6. Richard H. Stanley.

7. Radford University, Environmental History Timeline.

8. Keith Porter, "Global Leadership Requires Global Mandate," Courier Online, Fall 1999, <http://courier.stanleyfoundation.org/articles/1999fall1.html>

9. United Nations Environmental Programme, "The Johannesburg Declaration on Sustainable Development," September 4, 2002. <http://www.johannesburgsummit.org/html/documents/summit_docs/1009wssd_pol_declaration.doc>

10. The Environment Fund is the main source of funding for UNEP's activities.

11. United Nations Environmental Programme, "Financing UNEP," 2003. <http://www.unep.org/rmu/html/funding.htm>

Bibliography

Art, Robert J. and Robert Jervis, eds., *International Politics: Enduring Concepts and Contemporary Issues*, Third Edition (NY: Harper Collins Publishers, 1992)

Ausubel, Jesse "The Liberation of the Environment," *Daedalus* 125, 3 (1996): 1–7.

Ausubel, Jesse H., David G. Victor and Iddo K. Werneck, "The Environment since 1970," *Consequences: The Nature and Implications of Environmental Change 1*, no. 3 (1995): 2–15.

Axelrod, Robert and Robert Keohane, "Achieving Cooperation under Anarchy: Strategies and Limitations," in *Cooperation Under Anarchy*, ed. Kenneth Oye (Princeton: Princeton University Press, 1986)

Axelrod, Robert, *The Evolution of Cooperation* (Harmondsworth: Penguin Books, 1990)

Bachler, Gunther, *Occasional Paper No. 9: Conflict and Cooperation in the Light of Global Human-Ecological Transformation* (Zurich: Center for Security Studies and Conflict Research, 1993)

"Background to the United Nations Conference on Environment and Development" *The Globe*, 7 (1992)

Barber, Charles, *Global Environmental Security and International Cooperation: Conceptual, Organizational and Legal Framework* (Washington, D.C.: World Resources Institute, 1980)

Barkin, J. Samuel and George E. Shambaugh, eds. *Anarchy and the Environment: The International Relations of Common Pool Resources* (Albany: State University of New York Press, 1999)

Blodgett, John E., *Environmental Policy and the Economy: Conflicts and Concordances* (CRS Report 95–147 ENR) (US Library of Congress: Congressional Research Service, January 10, 1995)

Boldt Jr., J.R. and Queneau, P., *Winning of Nickel: Its Geology, Mining and Extractive Metallurgy* (Princeton, N.J.: D. Van Nostrand, 1967)

Bramble, Barbara J. and Gareth Porter, "Non-Governmental Organizations and the Making of US International Environmental Policy," in *The International Politics of the Environment*, eds. Andrew Hurrell and Benedict Kingsbury (Oxford: Oxford University Press, 1992): 313–354.

Brandt Commission, *North-South: A Programme for Survival*. (London: Pan Books, 1980)

Brent, Tony, *The Greening of Machiavelli: The Evolution of International Environmental Politics* (London Royal Institute of International Affairs, Energy, and Environmental Program: Earthscan Publications, 1994).

Brock, Lothar, "Environmental Degradation as a Security Issue: Conceptual Pitfalls and Empirical Challenges." Paper presented at the 16th General Conference of the International Peace Research Association, Brisbane Australia, 8–12 July 1996.

Brown, Lester R., et. al., *Worldwatch Institute: State of the World 1990* (NY: WW Norton, 1990).

Brown, Lester R., et. al., *Worldwatch Institute: State of the World 1991* (NY: WW Norton, 1991)

Brown, Lester R., et. al., *A Worldwatch Institute Report on Progress Toward Sustainable Development* (New York: Universe Books, 1991)

Brown, Lester R., et. al., *Worldwatch Institute: State of the World 1999* (N.Y.: W.W. Norton, 1999)

Brown, Lester R., et. al., *Vital Signs: The Environmental Trends that Are Shaping Our Future* (Worldwatch Institute, N.Y.: W.W. Norton, 1999)

Brown, Neville, "Climate, Ecology, and International Security," *Survival*, 31 no. 6 (1989): 519–532.

Bull, Hedley, *The Anarchical Society: A Study of Order in World Politics* (London: Macmillan, 1977)

Buzan, Barry, *Peoples, States and Fear: An Agenda for International Security Studies in the Post-Cold War Era*, Boulder (Colorado: Lynne Rienner, 1991)

Caldwell, Lynton, *International Environmental Policy*, (Durham: Duke University Press, 1984)

Cartledge, Bryan, ed., *Monitoring the Environment* (Oxford: Oxford University Press, 1992)

Central Intelligence Agency, *World Factbook* (Washington, D.C., 1988)

Committee for the National Institute for the Environment, *Cost-Benefit Analysis: Issues in Its Use in Regulation (CRS Report 95–760 ENR)* (US Library of Congress: Congressional Research Service, June 28, 1995)

Conca, Ken, "Global Environmental Governance: Causes, Components, and Consequences," Occasional Paper No. 6, (Harrison Program on the Future Global Agenda, 1995)

Conca, Ken and Ronnie D. Lipschutz, "A Tale of Two Forests," in *The State and Social Power in Global Environmental Politics*, eds. Ronnie D. Lipschutz and Ken Conca (N.Y.: Columbia University Press, 1993)

Cooley, J.K., "War over Water," *Foreign Policy* 54 (1984):3–26.

Dowdeswell, Elizabeth, "The Promise of Stockholm: UNEP 25," (Nairobi: United Nations Environmental Programme, 1997)

Doyle, Michael, "Liberalism and World Politics," APSR 86, no. 1 (1986)

Durham, W.H., *Scarcity and Survival in Central America: Ecological Origins of the Soccer War*, (Stanford: Stanford University Press, 1979)

Dyer, Hugh, "EcoCultures: Global Culture in the Age of Ecology," *Millennium: Journal of International Studies* 22, no. 3 (1993): 483–504.

Dyer, Hugh C., "Environmental Security as a Universal Value: Implications for International Theory," in *The Environment and International Relations*, eds. John Vogler and Mark Imbers (N.Y.: Routledge, 1996)

Earthwatch, Earthwatch: *1972–1992: A Review of the Development of Earthwatch* (Nairobi: United Nations Environmental Programme, 1992)

Eckes Jr., A.E., *United States and the Global Struggle for Minerals* (Austin: University of Texas Press, 1979)

Eckholm, Eric, *Down to Earth: Environment and Human Needs* (NY: W. W. Norton and Company, 1982)

Environment Canada, *The Changing Atmosphere: Implications for Global Security, Conference Statement* (Toronto, July 27–30, 1988)

"Environmental Problems: A Global Security Threat?" *Report of the 24th United Nations of the Next Decade Conference,* (New York, New York, June 18–23, 1989)

ESRC Global Environmental Change Programme, *Making Environmental Decisions: Cost-Benefit Analysis, Contingent Valuation and Alternatives, Center for the Study of Environmental Change and Green Practitioner's Seminar* (January 23, 1997)

Falk, Richard, "Democratizing, Internationalizing and Globalizing: A Collage of Blurred Images," *Changing World Order and the United Nations System,* (Yokohama, Japan, 1992)

Finger, Matthias, "The Military, the Nation State and the Environment," *The Ecologist* 21, no 5 (1991): 220–225.

Finkelstein, Lawrence S., "What is Global Governance?" *Global Governance* 1, no. 3 (1995): 369.

Fitzgerald, John M., "The Biological Diversity Treaty of the United Nations Conference on Environment and Development," *Endangered Species Update* 9, no. 9 and 10 (1992)

Florini, Ann, Julie Emmons and Laura Strohm, eds., *How Does Social Science Help Solve Environmental Problems,* (Los Angeles: University of California, 1992)

Freedom House, *Table of Independent Countries: Comparative Measures of Freedom,* 2000 <http://www.freedomhouse.org/>

Garcia, Rogelio, *Environmental Regulatory Reform: An Overview (CRS Issue Brief 95035),* US Library of Congress: Congressional Research Service.

Gleditsch, Nils Petter and Bjorn Otto Sverdrup, *Democracy and the Environment* (Oslo, Norway: International Peace Research Institute, 1996)

Glenn, John, "National Security: More Than Just Weapons Production," *Issues in Science and Technology* 5, no. 4 (1989): 27–28.

Golich, Vicki, *Instructors Manual: International Relations by Joshua Goldstein,* (NY: HarperCollins, 1994)

Goldstein, Joshua, *International Relations, Third Edition* (New York: Longman, 1999)

Gore, Al, "SEI: A Strategic Environment Initiative," *SAIS Review* 10, no. 1 (1991): 59–71.

Grieco, Joseph, "Anarchy and the Limits of Cooperation," *International Organization* 42, no. 3 (1988)

Grubb, Michael, "Global Environmental Change and International Agreements, Conventions and Protocols," *The Globe* 19 (1994)

Guruswamy, L.D., "Global Warming: Integrating United States and International Law," *Arizona Law Review* 32 (1990): 221–278.

Haas, Peter, "Conclusion: Epistemic Communities, World Order and the Creation of a Reflective Research Program," *International Organization* 46, no. 1 (1992): 367–390.

Haas, Peter M. and Ernst B. Haas, "Learning to Learn: Improving International Governance," *Global Governance* 1, no. 3 (1995): 255–284.

Haas, Peter, Marc Levy and Edward Parson, "How Should We Judge UNCED's Success?" *Environment* 34, no. 8 (1992)

Haas, Peter, Robert Keohane and Marc Levy, *Institutions for the Earth,* (Cambridge: MIT Press, 1993)

Halliday, Fred, "International Relations: Is There a New Agenda?" *Millennium* 20, no. 1(1991): 57–72.

Hankins, F.H., "Pressure of Population as a Cause of War," Annals of the *American Academy of Political and Social Science* 198 (1938):101–108.

Harris, Peter, Abraham Rotstein, and Peter Timmerman, "Nature's Veto: UNCED and the Debate over the Earth" (Working Group of Science for Peace: University of Toronto, 1992)

Harrison, S.S., *China, Oil and Asia: Conflict Ahead?* (N.Y. Columbia University Press, 1977)

Heinback, B., *Oil and Security* (Stockholm: Almquist and Wiksell, 1974)

Hempel, Lamont C., *Environmental Governance: the Global Challenge,* (Washington, D.C.: Island Press, 1996)

Herrera, Amilcar, et. al., *Catastrophe or New Society* (Ottowa: International Development Research Center, 1976)

Heseltine, Michael, "The Environment: A Political View," in Bryan Cartledge, ed., *Monitoring the Environment* (Oxford: Oxford University Press, 1992): 42–54.

Holdgate, Martin W., *A Perspective of Environmental Pollution* (Cambridge: Cambridge University Press, 1979)

Holdgate, Martin W., Mohammed Kassas, and Gilbert F. White, eds., *The World Environment 1972–1982* (Dublin: Tycooly International Publishing Limited, 1982)

Homer-Dixon, Thomas, "On the Threshold: Environmental Changes as Causes of Acute Conflicts," *International Security* 16, no. 2 (1991): 76–116.

Homer-Dixon, Thomas, "Environmental Scarcity and Global Security," *Foreign Policy Association,* 3000 (1993)

Homer-Dixon, Thomas, "Environmental Scarcities and Violent Conflict," *International Security* 19, no. 1 (1994): 5–40.

Homer-Dixon, Thomas, "Strategies for Studying Causation in Complex Ecological Political Systems," (Washington, D.C.: American Association for the Advancement of Science and the University of Toronto, 1995)

Homer-Dixon, Thomas F., Bartwell, Jeffrey H., and George H. Rathjens, "Environmental Change and Violent Conflict," *Scientific American* (1993): 38–45.

Hsiung, James C., *Anarchy and Order: The Interplay of Politics and Law in International Relations* (Boulder, Co.: Lynne Rienner, 1997)

Hughes, Barry B., *World Futures: A Critical Analysis of Alternatives* (Baltimore: John Hopkins University Press, 1985)

Huntington, Samuel P., *The Third Wave of Democratization in the Late 20th Century* (Norman, OK: University of Oklahoma Press, 1991)

Hurrell, Andrew and Benedict Kingsbury, eds., *The International Politics of the Environment* (Oxford: Oxford University Press, 1992)

Inglehart, Ronald, *The Silent Revolution: Changing Values and Political Styles Among Western Publics* (Princeton: Princeton University Press, 1977)

International Institute for Strategic Studies, *The Military Balance, 1992–1993* (London: International Institute for Strategic Studies, 1992)

International Labour Organization, *Yearbook of Labour Statistics* (Geneva, Switzerland: ILO, 1995)

Jacobson, Harold K. and Edith Brown Weiss, "Strengthening Compliance with International Environmental Accords: Preliminary Observations from a Collaborative Project," *Global Governance* 1 (1992): 119–148.

Jacobson, Harold K. and Edith Brown Weiss, "Compliance with International Environmental Accords: Achievements and Strategies," in *International Governance on Environmental Issues*. ed. Uno Svedin (Dodrecht, the Netherlands: Kluwer Academic Publishers, 1997)

Jeffreys, Kent, *Guide to Regulatory Reform: The Cost-Benefit Rule, Brief Analysis No. 150* (National Center for Policy Analysis: Dallas, Texas, 1995)

Jervis, Robert, "The Future of World Politics," *International Security* 16, no. 3 (1996)

Kahn, Herman, William Brown and Leon Martel, *The Next 200 Year* (N.Y. Morrow, 1976)

Kamenetsky, I., "Lebensraum in Hitler's War Plan: The Theory and Eastern European Reality," *American Journal of Economics and Sociology* 20 (1960–1961): 313–326.

Katzenstein, Peter J., ed., *The Culture of National Security: Norms and Identity in World Politics* (N.Y.: Columbia University Press, 1996)

Keller, Kenneth H, "Unpacking the Environment" in *Environmental Change and Security Project Report*, ed. P.J. Simmons (Woodrow Wilson Center: Washington, D.C., 1997): 5–14.

Keohane, Robert, *After Hegemony: Cooperation and Discord in the World Political Economy* (Princeton: Princeton University Press, 1984)

Keohane, Robert, *International Regimes* (Cornell: Cornell University Press, 1989)

Keohane, Robert, "A Functional Theory of Regimes," in *International Politics: Enduring Concepts and Contemporary Issues 3rd edition*, eds. Robert J. Art and Robert Jervis (NY: Harper Collins Publishers, 1992)

Keohane, Robert and Joseph Nye, *Power and Interdependence 2nd edition* (Boston: Little and Brown, 1989)

Kingdon, John, *Agendas, Alternatives, and Public Policies* (Boston: Brown and Company, 1984)

Klare, Michael T., "Redefining Security: The New Global Schisms," in *Perspective: Global Issues*, ed. James M. Lindsey. ed. (Boulder, CO: Coursewise Publishing, 1997): 2–7.

Krasner, Stephen, *International Regimes* (Ithaca: Cornell University Press, 1983)

Kruszewski, C., "Germany's Lebensraum," *APSR* 34 (1940): 964–975.

Lafferty, William, "Interview," *Natur & Miljo*, 1 (1993): 23–24.

Lake, David, "Anarchy, Hierarchy, and the Variety of International Relations," *International Organization* 50, no. 1 (1996)

Latham, Robert, "Thinking About Security after the Cold War," *International Studies Notes* 20, no. 3 (1995): 9–16.

Leith, C.K., *World Minerals and World Politics* (New York: McGraw-Hill, 1931)

Levy, Marc, "Is the Environment a National Security Issue?" *International Security* 20, no. 2 (1995): 35–62.

Levy, Mark, Robert Keohane, and Peter Haas, "Institutions for the Earth: Promoting International Environmental Protection," *Environment,* (1992): 12–17, and 29–36.

Liftin, Karen, "Eco-regimes: Playing Tug of War with the Nation-State," in *The State and Social Power in Global Environmental Politics,* eds. Ronnie D. Lipschutz and Ken Conca (New York: Columbia University Press, 1993)

Liftin, Karen, ed., *The Greening of Sovereignty in World Politics* (Cambridge: MIT Press, 1998)

Lindsey, James M., *Perspective: Global Issue* (Boulder, CO: Coursewise Publishing, 1997)

Lipschutz, Ronnie D. and Ken Conca, eds., (1993) *The State and Social Power in Global Environmental Politics,* New York: Columbia University Press, 1993

Lipschutz, Ronnie D., "From Place to Planet: Local Knowledge and Global Environmental Governance," *Global Governance* 3, no. 1 (1997): 83–102.

List, Martin and Volker Rittberger, "Regime Theory and International Environmental Management," in *The International Politics of the Environment,* eds. Andrew Hurrell and Benedict Kingsbury (Oxford: Oxford University Press, 1992): 85–109.

Lowi, Theodore, "American Business, Public Policy, Case-Studies, and Political Theory," *World Politics* 16 (1964)

Margulis, Sergio, "Environmental Regulation: Instruments and Actual Implementation" (Washington, D.C.: World Bank Environment Department, 1996)

Margulis, Sergio and Paulo Pereira de Gusmas, "Problems of Environmental Management in the Real World: The Rio de Janeiro Experience." (World Bank Environment Department, 1996)

Mathews, Jessica Tuchman, "Redefining Security," *Foreign Affairs* (1989)

McNeill, W.H., *Pursuit of Power: Technology, Armed Force, and Society Since A.D. 1000* (Chicago: University of Chicago Press, 1982)

Meadows, Donella H., Dennis L. Meadows, Jorgen Randers, and William W. Behrens, *The Limits to Growth: A Report for the Club of Rome's Project on the Predicament of Mankind* (N.Y.: Universe Books, 1972)

Mendez, Ruben P., "Paying for Peace and Development," *Foreign Policy* 100 (1995): 19–32.

Mesarovic, Mihajlo and Eduard Pestel, *Mankind at the Turning Point* (N.Y.: Dutton, 1974)

Middleton, Niels, Phil O'Keefe and Sam Moyo, *The Tears of the Crocodile: From Rio to Reality in the Developing World* (London: Pluto Press, 1993)

Midwest Consortium for International Security Studies and Argonne National Laboratory, *Global Climate Change and International Security Report on a Conference Held at Argonne National Laboratory* (1991)

Mitchell, B., "Politics, Fish and International Resource Management: the British-Icelandic Cod War," *Geographical Review* 66 (1976) 127–138.

Modelski, George, *Principles of World Politics* (N.Y.: Free Press, 1972)

Morgenthau, Hans, "Six Principles of Political Realism," in *Classical Readings of International Relations*, eds. Williams, Goldstein and Shafritz (Wadsworth, 1994)

Morowitz, Harold, "Balancing Species Preservation and Economic Considerations," *Science* 253, no. 5021 (1991)

Mungall, Constance and Degby J. McLaren, *The Challenge of Global Climate Change: Planet Under Stress* (Toronto: Oxford University Press, 1991)

Myers, Norman, "Environment and Security," Foreign Policy 74 (1989): 23–41.

New Comparative World Atlas (N.Y.: Hammond, 1998)

Nye, Joseph S., "The Changing Nature of World Power," *Political Science Quarterly* 105, no. 2 (1990)

Olson Jr., Mancur, *The Logic of Collective Action* (Cambridge Massachusetts: Harvard University Press, 1971)

Ostrom, Elinor, *Governing the Commons: The Evolution of Institutions for Collective Action* (N.Y.: Cambridge University Press, 1990)

Ophuls, William, *Ecology and the Politics of Scarcity: Prologue to a Political Theory of the Steady State* (San Francisco: Freeman, 1977)

Organski, A.F.K., Bruce Bueno de Mesquita and Alan Lamborn, "The Effective Population in International Politics," in *Governance and Population: The Governmental Implications of Population Change*, ed. A.E. Keir Nash (1992): 237–249.

Organski, A.F.K. and Jacek Kugler, *The War Ledger* (Chicago: Chicago University Press, 1980)

Oye, Kenneth, "The Conditions for the Cooperation in World Politics" in *International Politics: Enduring Concepts and Contemporary Issues, Third Edition*, eds., Robert J. Art and Robert Jervis (NY: Harper Collins Publishers, 1992)

Park, C.H., "South China Sea Disputes: Who Owns the Islands and the Natural Resources?" *Ocean Development and International Law* 5 (1978): 27–59.

Parker, Jonathan, "The State of the Environment," *Environment* 34, no. 1 (1992)

Passmore, John, *Man's Responsibility for Nature* (London: Duckworth, 1974)

Payne, Rodger A., "Freedom and the Environment," *Journal of Democracy* 6, no. 3 (1995): 41–55.

Peluso, Nancy Lee, "Coercing Conservation: The Politics of State Resource Control," in *The State and Social Power in Global Environmental Politics*, eds., Ronnie D. Lipschutz and Ken Conca (New York: Columbia University Press, 1993)

Pearce, David, Edward Barbier, and Anil Markandya, *Sustainable Development: Economics and the Environment in the Third World* (London: Edward Elgar, 1990)

"Persuasion and Incentives: New Ways to Achieve a Cleaner World," *Environment Matters* (1997)

Phillipson, John, "The natural world: a global casino," in *Monitoring the Environment*, ed., Bryan Cartledge (Oxford: Oxford University Press, 1992): 193–206.

Pirages, Dennis Clark, *Global Ecopolitics: A New Context for International Relations* (North Scituate: Duxbury Press, 1978)

Pirages, Dennis Clark, *Global Technopolitics: The International Politics of Technology and Resources* (Pacific Grove: Brooks/Cole Publishing Company, 1989)

Pirages, Dennis Clark, "Social Evolution and Ecological Security," *Bulletin of Peace Proposals* 22 (1991): 329–334.

Pirages, Dennis Clark, "The Greening of Peace Research," *Journal of Peace Research* 28, no. 2 (1991): 129–133.

Porter, Gareth and Janet Welsh Brown, *Global Environmental Politics* (Boulder: Westview Press, 1991)

Powell, Robert, "Absolute and Relative Gains in International Relations Theory," *American Political Science Review* 85, no. 4 (1991): 1303–1320.

Powell, Robert, "What is/Is Not Distinctive About Environmental Questions" in *How Does Social Science Help Solve Environmental Problems,* eds. Florini, Ann, Julie Emmons and Laura Strohm (Los Angeles: University of California, 1992): 31–34.

Rae, Heather and Chris Reus-Smit, eds., *The United Nations: Between Sovereignty and Global Governance?* (Melbourne: La Trobe University, 1995)

Regens, James L. and Robert W. Rycroft, *The Acid Rain Controversy* (Pittsburgh: University of Pittsburgh Press, 1988)

Renner, Michael, "Assessing the Military's War on the Environment," in *State of the World,* Lester Brown, et. al. (N.Y.: Norton, 1991): 137–138.

Renner, Michael, *Fighting for Survival: Environmental Decline, Social Conflict, and the New Age of Insecurity* (N.Y.: Worldwatch Institute, 1996)

Repetto, Robert and Jonathan Lash, "Planetary Roulette: Gambling with the Climate," in *Perspective: Global Issues,* ed. James M. Lindsey (Boulder, CO: Coursewise Publishing, 1997): 44–50.

Richardson, L. F., *Statistics of Deadly Quarrels* (Pittsburgh: Boxwood Press, 1969)

Roodman, David Malin, "Building a Sustainable Society," in *Worldwatch Institute: State of the World 1999,* Lester Brown, et. al. (N.Y.: W.W. Norton, 1999): 169–188.

Romm, Joseph J., *Defining National Security: The Non-Military Aspects* (N. Y.: Council on Foreign Relations Press, 1993)

Rosenau, James N., "Governance, Order and Change in World Politics," in *Governance Without Government: Order and Change in World Politics,* eds. James N. Rosenau and Ernst-Otto Czempiel (Cambridge: Cambridge University Press, 1992)

Rosenau, James N., "Environmental Challenges in a Turbulent World," in *The State and Social Power in Global Environmental Politics,* eds. Ronnie D. Lipschutz and Ken Conca (New York: Columbia University Press, 1993)

Russett, Bruce, "Security and the Resources Scramble: Will 1984 be Like 1914?" *International Affairs* 58 (1981–1982): 42–58.

Russett, Bruce, "Peace between Participatory Polities," *World Politics* 44 (1992): 573–599.

Russett, Bruce, *Grasping Democratic Peace: Principles for a Post-Cold War World* (Princeton: Princeton University Press, 1993)

Russett, Bruce, J.D. Singer, and Melvin Small, "National Political Units in the 20th Century: A Standardized List," APSR 62, no. 4 (1968): 932–951.

Russett, Bruce and Harvey Starr, *World Politics: The Menu for Choice* (NY: W.H. Freeman, 1996)

Safran N., *From War to War: the Arab-Israeli Confrontation, 1948–1967* (N.Y.: Pegasus, 1969)

Salamon, Lester M. and Helmet K. Anheir, *The Emerging Sector Revisited: A Summary of Initial Estimates* (Baltimore: John Hopkins University Center for Civil Society Studies, 1998)

Sandbrook, Richard, "Down to Earth: Five Years from Rio," in *Perspective: Global Issue,* ed. James M. Lindsey (Boulder, CO: Coursewise Publishing, 1997): 212–215.

Sanger, Clyde, *Ordering the Oceans: The Making of the Law of the Sea* (London: Zed Books, 1986)

Schierow, Linda-Jo, *The Role of Risk Analysis and Risk Management in Environmental Protection* (94036) (Washington, D.C.: Committee for the National Institute for the Environment, 1997)

Schrijver, Nico, *Sovereignty Over Natural Resources: Balancing of Rights and Duties* (Cambridge, U.K.: Cambridge University Press, 1997)

Simon, Julian, *The Ultimate Resource* (Princeton: Princeton University Press, 1981)

Simon, Julian and Herman Kahn, *The Resourceful Earth* (Oxford: Blackwell, 1984)

Singer, J. David and Melvin Small, *National Material Capabilities Data Set* (1993)

Singer, Max, *Passage to a Human World* (Indianapolis: Hudson Institute, 1987)

Sitarz, Daniel, Agenda 21 (Boulder, Colorado: Earthpress, 1993)

Skocpol, Theda, "Bringing the State Back In: Strategies of Analysis in Current Research," in *Bringing the State Back In,* eds. Peter Evans, Dietrich Rueschemeyer, and Theda Skocpol (Cambridge: Cambridge University Press, 1985)

Snidal, Duncan, "Relative Gains and the Pattern of International Cooperation," *International Organization* 85, no. 3 (1991): 701–726.

Snow, Donald M. and Eugene Brown, *Puzzle Palaces and Foggy Bottom: U.S. Foreign and Defense Policy-Making in the 1990s* (N.Y.: St. Martin Press, 1994)

Soroos, Marvin, "Global Change, Environmental Security, and the Prisoner's Dilemma," *Journal of Peace Research* 31, no. 3, (1994): 317–332.

Southwood, Richard, "The environment: problems and prospects," in *Monitoring the Environment,* ed. Bryan Cartledge (Oxford: Oxford University Press, 1992): 5–41.

Sprinz, Detlef, *Regulating the International Environment: A Conceptual Model of Environmental Security and Instrument Choice* (Potsdam: Potsdam Institute for Climate Impact Research, 1995)

Sprinz, Detlef and Tapani Vaahtoranta, "The Interest-Based Explanation for International Air Pollution Control: Determinants of Support for the Protection of the Ozone Layer and the Abatement of Acid Rain in Europe," in *The International Politics of Environmental Management,* ed. Arild Underdal (Dordrecht: Kluwer Academic Publishers, 1993).

Stein, Arthur, "Coordination and Collaboration: Regimes in an Anarchic World," in *International Regimes,* ed. Stephan Krasner (Ithaca, N.Y.: Cornell University Press, 1983)

Strange, Susan, "Cave! Hic Dragones: A Critique of Regime Analysis," *International Organization* 32, no. 2 (1982): 479–493.

Strong, Maurice F., The Way Ahead: *UNEP 25* (Nairobi: United Nations Environmental Programme, 1997)

Subramanian, Uma and Julian A. Lampietti, *Taking Stock of National Environmental Strategies* (edp1009) (Washington, D.C.: World Bank Land, Water and Natural Habitats Division, 1995)

Susskind, Lawrence and Connie Ozawa, "Negotiating More Effective International Environmental Agreements," in *The International Politics of the Environment,* eds. Andrew Hurrell and Benedict Kingsbury (Oxford: Oxford University Press, 1992): 142–165.

Switzer, Jacqueline Vaughn with Gary Bryner, *Environmental Politics: Domestic and Global Dimensions 2nd edition* (New York: St. Martin's Press, 1998)

Tolba, Mostafa K., ed., *Evolving Environmental Perceptions: From Stockholm to Nairobi* (London: Butterworths, 1988)

Tolba, Mostafa K., Osama A. El-kholy, M.W. Holdgate, D.F. McMichael, and R.E. Munn, eds., *The World Environment 1972–1992: Two Decades of Challenge* (London: Chapman and Hall, 1992)

Tolba, Mostafa K. and Iwona Rummel-Bulska, *Global Environmental Diplomacy: Negotiating Environmental Agreements for the World 1973–1992* (Cambridge: MIT Press, 1998)

Union of International Associations, *The Yearbook of International Organizations* (Brussels: Union of International Associations, 1997)

United Nations, *International Environmental Conflict Resolution* (N.Y.: United Nations Publications, 1992)

United Nations, *World Population Prospects: The 1996 Revision* (N.Y.: United Nations, 1996)

United Nations, *U.N. Register of International Treaties and Other Agreements in the Field of the Environment* (2002)

United Nation Commission on Permanent Sovereignty Over Natural Resources *GAR* 1803 [XVII] (1962)

United Nations Development Programme, *Human Development Report* 1993 (New York: Oxford University Press, 1993)

United Nations Development Programme, *Human Development Report 1994* (Cambridge, Mass: Basil Blackwell Inc., 1994): 229–236.

United Nations Environmental Programme, *The Public and the Environment* (Nairobi: United Nations Environmental Programme, 1988)

United Nations Environmental Programme, Environmental Data Report 1989 (Cambridge, Mass.: Basil Blackwell Inc., 1989)

United Nations Environmental Programme, "World Wide Concern about the Environment," *Our Planet* (Nairobi: United Nations Environmental Programme, 1989)

United Nations Environmental Programme, *Environmental Data Report 1991* (Oxford: Basil Blackwell Ltd, 1991)

United Nations Environmental Programme, *Environmental Data Report 1991* (Oxford: Basil Blackwell Ltd., 1991)

United Nations Environmental Programme, *Global Environmental Outlook–1, "Overview of Regional Status and Trends"* (1997) <http://grid2.cr.usgs.gov/geo1/exsumm/ex3.htm>

United Nations Environmental Programme, *Our Planet 8.5* (1997) <http://www.ourplanet.com/txtversn/85/contents.html>

United Nations Population Division and Statistics Division of the United Nations Secretariat, *Indicators on Population* (1997)

United Nations Press Release ORG/1190 (December 15, 1994)

United Nations Secretariat, *United Nations Member States* (1997)

United States Bureau of the Census, *World Population Profile* (Washington, D.C.: US Printing Office, 1996)

Vienna Convention on the Law of Treaties (1969)

Von Prittwitz, Volker, "Several Approaches to the Analysis of International Environmental Policy," in *Maintaining A Satisfactory Environment,* ed. Nordal Akerman (Boulder, Colorado: Westview Press, 1990)

Wapner, Paul, "Reorienting State Sovereignty: Rights and Responsibilities in the Environmental Age," in *The Greening of Sovereignty in World Politics,* ed. Karen Liftin (Cambridge: MIT Press, 1998): 275–297.

Walt, Stephan, *The Origins of Alliances* (Ithaca, N.Y.: Cornell University Press, 1987)

Waltz, Kenneth, *Theory of International Politics* (Addison-Wesley, 1979)

Wendt, Alexander, "Anarchy Is What States Make of It," *International Organization* 46, no. 2 (1992): 391–425.

Westing, Arthur, ed., *Global Resources and International Conflict: Environmental Factors in Strategic Policy and Action* (Oxford: Oxford University Press, 1986)

White, Rodney, *North, South, and the Environmental Crisis,* Toronto: University of Toronto Press, 1993)

Wijkman, Per Magnus, "Managing the Global Commons," *International Organization,* 36, no. 3 (1982)

Wooley, Wesley T., *Alternatives to Anarchy: American Supranationalism Since World War II* (Bloomington: Indiana University Press, 1988)

World Bank, World *Development Report 1991: The Challenge of Development* (Oxford: Oxford University Press, 1991)

World Bank, *World Tables 1991* (Baltimore: John Hopkins University Press, 1991)

World Bank, *Social Indicators of Development 1991–1992* (Baltimore: John Hopkins University Press, 1992)

World Bank, *World Development Report 1992: Development and the Environment* (Oxford: Oxford University Press, 1992)

World Bank, *The World Bank and the Environment* (Washington, DC: The World Bank, 1993)

World Bank, World *Development Report 1993: Investing in Health* (Oxford: Oxford University Press, 1993)

World Bank, World *Development Report 1997: The State In a Changing World* (New York: Oxford University Press, 1997)

World Bank, *Environment Matters* (Washington: World Bank, 1997)

World Commission on Environment and Development, *Our Common Future* (Oxford: Oxford University Press, 1987)

World Conservation Union, United Nations Environmental Programme, and World Wildlife Fund for Nature, *Caring for Earth: A Strategy for Sustainable Living* (Gland, Switzerland: World Conservation Union, 1991)

World Resources Institute, *World Resources 1992–1993* (NY: Oxford University Press, 1992)

World Resources Institute, *World Resources 1994–1995* (NY: Oxford University Press. 1994)

World Resources Institute, *World Resources 1996–1997* (N.Y.: Oxford University Press, 1996)

Wyller, Thomas, "The Ecological Crisis: A Problem of Democratic Political Power," Paper presented at the 16th World Congress of Political Science, Berlin, 21–25 August, 1994.

Young, Oran, "International Regimes: Toward a New Theory of Institutions," *World Politics,* 39 (1986)

Young, Oran, "The Politics of International Regime Formation: Managing Natural Resources and the Environment," *International Organization* 43 (1989): 349–375.

Young, Oran, *International Governance: Protecting the Environment in a Stateless Society* (Ithaca: Cornell University Press, 1994)

Zook Jr., D.H., *Conduct of the Chaco War.* (N.Y.: Bookman, 1960)

Index